Orchids

Orchids

Essential know-how and expert advice for gardening success

CONTENTS

WHAT ARE ORCHIDS?

Orchids are among the most fascinating plants on the planet. Their flowers have evolved—hand in hand with their pollinators—into myriad forms, so orchids now display the widest diversity of any plant family. They occupy many ecological niches, living high up in the branches of trees in tropical forests, as well as in boggy temperate lowlands. They were first sought out by intrepid plant hunters, often at a cost to the environment that was not fully appreciated at the time. Modern conservation programs and production techniques have brought a vast range of orchids to the attention of the public, making these plants more popular than ever before.

WHY GROW ORCHIDS?

Orchids have a unique appeal. Exotic, flamboyant, even bizarre, no other plant family exhibits such a diversity of flower forms and colors. For many years, they were the province of collectors and connoisseurs who had the time and money to cater to the plants' specific needs. However, modern breeding and production techniques have brought them within reach of any plant enthusiast. Orchids now number among the easiest to grow of flowering house plants, are readily available, and make ideal gifts, lasting much longer than a bunch of flowers or box of chocolates.

The monkey orchid, *Dracula simia*, exemplifies the amazing flower forms that have evolved in this plant family.

THE APPEAL OF ORCHIDS

Almost everything about orchids is fascinating—from the strange way in which many of them grow, perching high in tree tops, stretching upward toward the light, or scrabbling over rocks, to their flowers, which take on so many strange and intricate forms. The blooms can be packed densely on the stems, or held aloft in airy, open clusters, hovering above a plant like a swarm of insects. With more than 100,000 hybrids available in a multitude of colors, there is an orchid to satisfy every taste, and you only need experience of growing one or two before you're hooked for life.

ORCHIDS FOR EVERYONE

Back in the 19th and early 20th centuries, when orchids began to be bought and sold, they were expensive and could be grown only in heated conservatories or in glass tanks in which rainforest conditions could be simulated.

Today, however, plant breeders have produced a huge range of plants that are perfectly happy in the average, centrally heated living room. No longer rare, but still precious to those who have succumbed to their charms, orchids are affordable and can be successfully grown by anyone.

Phalaenopsis (moth orchids) are the most widely available on the market.

The naked man orchid (*Orchis italica*) is named for its lobed lips, which resemble a human figure.

ORCHIDS IN THE WILD

There are around 25,000 species of orchids, making the Orchidaceae one of the largest of plant families, accounting for some 10 percent of all flowering plants. It is impossible to pin down the exact number of species because new plants continue to be discovered while others are lost, chiefly through the destruction of their habitats. Orchids grow naturally on every continent except Antarctica and have adapted to a wide range of conditions, growing from sea level to high up in mountainous regions, and from cool European meadowlands to tropical rainforests.

ORCHID HABITATS

While orchids as a family are widely distributed, individual species usually occupy narrow ecological niches—they thrive in very specific conditions. Orchids of the northern temperate zone (where there are cold winters in which temperatures drop below freezing) are usually found in bogs, prairies, and deciduous forests; most are terrestrial, rooting in the ground like other plants. However, the majority of orchid species are native to the tropics. Here, most grow epiphytically (see *box, right*); a few are lithophytic (from the Greek *lithos*, meaning "rock"), growing in the cracks between rocks, or terrestrial. They are often found in dense forest on mountainsides where cloud cover is virtually constant. The slope of the ground allows light to penetrate the leaf canopy, greatly benefiting the orchids. They are seldom found on areas of flat ground.

Orchids that grow on high mountains favor cool conditions, while those nearer sea level thrive in higher temperatures. Knowledge of the natural habitats of orchids provides growers with valuable clues about how to raise them in cultivation.

The vast majority of orchids available for sale have their origins in the forests of the tropics.

ORCHIDS AND PLANT EVOLUTION

In evolutionary terms, orchids are among the youngest members of the plant kingdom. They have developed specialized ways of growing and reproducing. In the wild, each species only thrives in very specific conditions and relies on a particular species of pollinator, which is usually an insect but sometimes a bat or even a bird, that may itself be endemic to a particular geographic area. There is often a mutual dependence between a plant and its pollinator. Some orchid flowers mimic the scent or appearance of the females of certain insect species so they can attract males that transfer pollen grains to neighboring plants, ensuring fertilization takes place and seed is produced.

Orchids rely on very specific pollinators that may themselves be under threat of local extinction.

Epiphytic orchids, such as this dendrobium, use their roots to cling to tree branches.

WHAT IS AN EPIPHYTE?

From the Greek *epi* (meaning "upon") and *phytos* ("plant"), an epiphyte is a plant that grows on the surface of another plant—usually a tree—rather than rooted in the ground. The epiphytic habit is seen in some mosses, lichens, algae, ferns, bromeliads, and, of course, orchids.

Epiphytes are not parasites. They take no nutrients from their host plant but use it only for physical support. They make energy by photosynthesis and derive mineral nutrients from rainfall or atmospheric mists.

Orchids that grow in the clefts between tree branches often have their roots covered by scraps of shed bark and leaves; this creates a growing medium that mimics the litter that collects around the base of the tree trunk. Hence some orchids are capable of growing both on trees as epiphytes and at their feet as terrestrials—the conditions are not markedly different.

ORCHIDS UNDER THREAT

With their reliance on specific pollinators and their dependence on a narrow set of environmental conditions, orchids are vulnerable to any changes in their habitat or broader ecosystem. Disturbance, clearing for agriculture and forestry, and climate change continue to place species under threat. Many have become extinct in the wild and are maintained only in botanic gardens. The collection of orchids from the wild has been banned in most countries, and in many parts of the world plant biologists are reintroducing orchids into their natural habitats. However, these programs are not straightforward because they depend on meeting the tough germination requirements of orchid seeds (see p.42).

(see p.42)

Pink lady slipper orchids are under threat in the US from clear-cutting, development, and poaching.

ORCHID HISTORY

Orchids were known to Chinese herbalists more than 3,000 years ago, and in the 5th century BCE were named "King of Fragrant Plants" by the philosopher Confucius. Valued for their beauty, scent, and medicinal qualities by civilizations including the ancient Greeks and the Aztecs, orchids became popular with gardeners in the western world in relatively recent times. Even in the 18th century, they were rarely seen outside botanical gardens that were the domain of collectors and connoisseurs.

The Temperate House at The Royal Botanic Gardens in Kew, London, holds part of the Gardens' collection of almost 5,000 orchids.

EARLY INTEREST

Orchids were cultivated for use in Chinese and South Asian Ayurvedic traditional medicine many centuries ago, and food products such as vanilla and salep (a drink that first became popular in the Ottoman empire) have long been produced from the plants.

Horticulturalists in Europe had their interest in orchids awakened after the introduction of tropical species from Mexico, Panama, and Venezuela. It is thought that *Brassavola nodosa* was first grown in the Netherlands toward the end of the 17th century and *Bletia purpurea*—a terrestrial orchid from the Bahamas—was one of the first to be imported into Britain. By 1789, the collection of exotic orchids held by what is now the Royal Botanic Gardens at Kew numbered just 15.

WHAT'S IN A NAME?

The Greek philosopher and naturalist Theophrastus (c. 371–c. 287 BCE) referred to orchids in his *Historia Plantarum* (*Inquiry Into Plants*), naming them *orkhis* (Greek for "testicle"), alluding to the shape of their pseudobulbs. Crushed and eaten, these were believed to increase male potency. In modern medicine, orchitis is the name for inflammation of the testicles.

The frontispiece to an illustrated 1644 edition of *Historia Plantarum*.

The lady of the night orchid (*Brassavola nodosa*) was brought to Europe from Curaçao in the Caribbean in 1698.

ORCHIDOMANIA

Cattleya labiata was discovered in Brazil in 1816.

The 17th century phenomenon of tulipomania—when tulip bulbs were bought and sold for hugely inflated sums—is well documented. Less familiar though is the similar craze for orchids that exploded in the early 19th century. At that time, naturalists had started exploring tropical regions, sending the specimens they collected back to their patrons in Europe, among whom was avid horticulturalist William Cattley of Barnet, north London. Cattley became the first person to successfully grow a tropical orchid in the British climate; the plant was later named *Cattleya labiata* in his honor. His success inspired huge interest, and tropical orchids became status symbols for the wealthy. Plant hunters were sent out to look for more, which resulted in hundreds of thousands of orchids being taken from the wild.

A DESTRUCTIVE TRADE

Driven by orchidomania and the growth of empires that encompassed the far-flung tropics, plant collectors expanded their searches. It was a dangerous pursuit that involved journeying into unmapped terrain. When orchids were spotted—often high up in the tree canopy—large areas of forest were felled so the plants could easily be gathered. The plant hunters collected all they could carry and would often destroy the plants that they could not transport to frustrate their competitors. Many orchids were driven to extinction as their habitat was destroyed. The high costs involved in mounting such campaigns meant that the price of the plants was correspondingly high, making them affordable only by the wealthiest gardeners.

Tissue culture was key to expanding demand for orchids, but required new growing techniques.

LATER DEVELOPMENTS

The first tropical orchids to be imported to Europe relied on hothouses to survive, but the discovery of cooler growing species, such as *Oncidium alexandrae* in Colombia, made orchids more accessible to the wider public. However, propagation from seed proved tricky and it was only in 1922 that Dr. Lewis Knudson of Cornell University in New York succeeded in creating a synthetic gel that allowed germination in the laboratory. Breeders realized that orchids would hybridize freely, and the range of cultivars grew rapidly. Today, orchids are propagated by a laboratory process called tissue culture, whereby vast quantities of plants can be produced at low cost.

Mountainous areas of Brazil were among those worst damaged by plant hunters.

ORCHID BIOLOGY AND NAMING

Orchids are perennials—they live for several years (up to 25 for some species) and bloom every year. Some, including almost all the commonly grown tropical orchids, are evergreens, while others are herbaceous, dying back for a period—usually over winter—each year. Orchids are unlike many garden and indoor plants in their growth forms, flower structures, and the way they are named. Much of the jargon required to understand orchid growth and naming is explored below.

MONOPODIAL AND SYMPODIAL ORCHIDS

Orchid plants grow in one of two basic forms—monopodial and sympodial. Monopodial orchids have one upright-growing stem from which the leaves arise in an alternate pattern. Flower stems emerge from the leaf bases, and aerial roots may form on the upper part of the stem. These roots allow plants to attach to tree trunks and reach the tree canopy.

Sympodial orchids have a thick horizontal stem, or rhizome, close to or under the ground. The rhizome produces successive growths from one end, extending the plant progressively sideways. These growths are called pseudobulbs and they carry the orchid's leaves. Pseudobulbs are swollen, upright stems that store water and food to nourish the plant while it is dormant. Most are oval to rounded or pear-shaped and can be up to 4 in (10 cm) long.

Sympodial orchids produce at least one new pseudobulb each year, but sometimes more. Pseudobulbs outlive the foliage they carry, which dies back after three or four years. At this point pseudobulbs become known as "back bulbs": these supply nutrients to newer flower- and leaf-bearing pseudobulbs, before withering entirely. Only young pseudobulbs on the growing edge of the plant produce flower spikes, either from the base or the tip.

Monopodial orchid

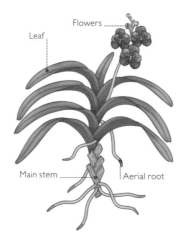

Flowers

Leaf

Main stem

Aerial root

Sympodial orchid

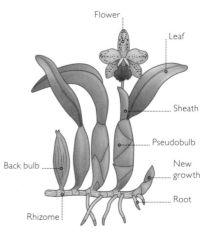

Flower

Leaf

Sheath

Pseudobulb

New growth

Back bulb

Root

Rhizome

Monopodial orchids are native to dense, misty rainforests at higher altitudes.

Sympodial orchids usually grow in rainforests at sea level or low altitudes.

The roots of this epiphytic orchid cling to a tree branch.

AERIAL ROOTS

While the roots of terrestrial orchids anchor the plant in the ground, the roots of epiphytes (see p.11) attach the orchid to its host plant (or rock, in the case of lithophytes) and are constantly exposed to light and the air. These aerial roots are an excellent indicator of the plant's health; they should be firm and pale in color. After a period of dormancy, roots that show green at their tips indicate that the plant is coming back into growth.

HOW ORCHIDS ARE NAMED

Like all living things, orchids are named according to the binomial (two name) system devised by Swedish botanist Carl Linnaeus (1707–78). The crimson cattleya orchid, *Cattleya labiata,* for example, belongs to the genus *Cattleya* and has the species name *labiata*; these names are always set in italic type.

Species within one genus sometimes interbreed to produce hybrids that are more robust and have larger flowers than their parents. While this can occur in the wild, most orchid hybrids available to buy are the result of deliberate crossing by orchid breeders.

HYBRID GROUPS When two orchids are crossed, the result is a group of hybrid plants, or *grex* (the Latin word for "flock"). This hybrid group is given a unique name, for example *Cymbidium* Kings Loch. Here, *Cymbidium* (set in italics) is the name of the genus, while Kings Loch (set in plain type with capital letters) is the name of the *grex*, or hybrid group.

A cross between two naturally occurring species is known as a primary hybrid. These primary hybrids can, in turn, be crossed with other primary hybrids, or with species plants, to create complex hybrids. Many of the orchids for sale today are members of complex hybrid groups.

CULTIVARS Occasionally, one of the seedlings resulting from a cross will display a particularly desirable characteristic that distinguishes it from other members of its hybrid group and will be given a unique cultivar name. This name is signaled by the use of single inverted quotes, for example *Cymbidium* Kings Loch 'Cooksbridge Noel' is a selected cultivar of the hybrid group Kings Loch. The parentage of all orchid hybrids is recorded in the International Orchid Register (IOR), searchable online.

HYBRID GENERA Plants from different genera do not normally hybridize because they are too distant genetically. Orchids are an exception. Their interbreeding has resulted in several hybrid genera. *Rhyncholaeliocattleya*, for example, is a result of crossing *Cattleya* and *Rhyncholaelia*. Hybrid genera are signaled by a cross "×" before the name (hence × *Rhyncholaeliocattleya* is correct), but the "×" is often omitted.

***Cymbidium* Kings Loch** is a complex hybrid that was registered in 1985.

ORCHID FLOWERS

The huge diversity of orchid flowers is a large part of what makes this plant family so fascinating. Flowers of some species can be studied only under a magnifying glass, while others, with elongated "tails," span up to 15 in (38 cm). Orchid flowers all share the same basic structure but individual parts vary between species and cultivars. Almost all colors are represented, and flowers are often strikingly marked and patterned. Many are waxy in texture, while others are more delicate or gleam like polished glass.

The lips of orchid flowers are often exquisitely marked and colored in contrast to the petals and sepals.

STRUCTURE

A typical orchid flower is symmetrical about its vertical axis and made up of distinct segments. Outermost are three sepals that serve to protect the developing flower bud. When the flower opens, the sepals expand and become colored and patterned. The topmost (dorsal) sepal may become particularly showy, and in some orchids the sepals are even more highly decorated than the petals.

Two petals flank the lip, which is itself a modified petal. The lip serves as a landing platform for insects that visit to pollinate the flower and is sometimes the showiest part of the bloom. Lips have various shapes and embellishments, and are sometimes inflated to form a pouch, as in the so-called "slipper orchids," the paphiopedilums and phragmipediums. The reproductive components of the flower that hold the pollen-bearing structures and female parts are located in a projection called the column. The anther cap at the end of the column is thought to prevent self-pollination of the flower.

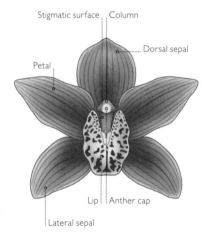

Stigmatic surface Column

Petal

Dorsal sepal

Lip Anther cap

Lateral sepal

ATTRACTING POLLINATORS

The wide range of orchid flower forms and colors reflects how each species has developed its own strategy to attract pollinators. White flowers with a strong scent—usually sweet or musky—are typical of orchids that are pollinated by nocturnal insects, principally moths. Butterflies that are active by day prefer brightly colored flowers that are often also fragrant.

Bird-pollinated flowers are strongly colored in reds, blues, and yellows, but are usually scentless, as birds have little sense of smell. Flowers in the dull green, brown, purple, or red range sometimes smell of rotting meat or dung to appeal to flies, which are also drawn to flowers with long tails at the ends of petals that wave in the air. The lines and other markings on flowers direct pollinators toward the pollen grains that are located at the center of the flower.

A bee orchid imitates a female bee, attracting males as pollinators.

This Ecuadorian orchid is pollinated by a hummingbird—the purple-bibbed whitetip.

FLOWERS FOR EVERY SEASON

Among the many attractions of orchids is that—with judicious choice of species—you can have plants in flower virtually every day of the year. Many of the most widely available orchids, such as phalaenopsis, dendrobiums, and cymbidiums, will flower for weeks, if not months, at a time. Some flower at a specific time of year (even winter), while others produce their blooms at almost any time. To help you plan your orchid year, the lists below give the flowering times of all the orchids described in this book and the temperatures under which they thrive (see p.34).

ANY TIME OF YEAR

Some orchids flower intermittently, often with gaps of several months between flowering. They may not flower at the same time from one year to the next.

COOL GROWING *Dracula vampira* • *Maxillaria variabilis* • *Oncidium*: Mount Bingham; Sharry Baby
INTERMEDIATE GROWING *Coelogyne speciosa* • *Miltonia* Sunset • *Paphiopedilum* Pinocchio
WARM GROWING *Phalaenopsis*: *cornu-cervi*; Lundy

ALL YEAR

These orchids produce a seemingly endless succession of flowers, new clusters appearing as older ones fade. They need resting occasionally (see p.35).

COOL GROWING *Epidendrum* × *obrienianum* • *Psychopsis papilio*
INTERMEDIATE GROWING *Epidendrum radicans* • *Phragmipedium* Sedenii • *Prosthechea cochleata*
WARM GROWING *Phalaenopsis*: Allegria; Doris; Golden Horizon 'Sunrise'; Lipperose

SPRING

Many orchids are spring flowering, the buds often forming in late winter at the end of dormancy. Start watering and feeding regularly once the buds appear.

COOL GROWING *Anguloa clowesii* • *Bletilla*: *ochracea*; *striata* • *Brassia*: Arania Verde; *aurantiaca*; Rex • *Calanthe*: *discolor*; *striata* • *Cattleya*: Chic Bonnet; *maxima*; *trianae* • *Cattlianthe* Hazel Boyd 'Apricot Glow' • *Coelogyne*: *cristata*; *flaccida* • *Cymbidium*: Castle of Mey 'Pinkie'; *devonianum*; *erythrostylum*; *insigne* 'Mrs Carl Holmes'; Showgirl • *Dendrobium*: *aphyllum*; Berry 'Oda'; *chrysanthum*; Happiness; *infundibulum*; 'Irene Smile'; Momozomo 'Princess'; *nobile*; Oriental Paradise; Spiral Gem 'Universal Topaz'; Spring Dream 'Apollon'; *victoriae-reginae*; *williamsonii* • *Dracula bella* • *Lycaste*: *aromatica*; *cruenta*; *deppei* • *Masdevallia wagneriana* • *Maxillaria porphyrostele* • *Oncidium*: Jungle Monarch; *lanceanum* • *Paphiopedilum venustum* • *Pleione*: Alishan 'Merlin'; *bulbocoides*; *formosana*; Shantung 'Silver Anniversary'
INTERMEDIATE GROWING *Bulbophyllum ambrosia* • *Cattleya leopoldii* • *Coelogyne mooreana* 'Westonbirt' • *Dendrobium*: *kingianum*; *macrophyllum*; 'Polar Fire'; *polysema* • *Paphiopedilum*: *appletonianum*; *armeniacum*; *bellatum*; *callosum*; *concolor*; *delenatii*; Goultenianum 'Album'; *haynaldianum*; Maudiae 'Coloratum'; Miller's Daughter; *rothschildianum*; Vanda M. Pearman; *villosum* • *Phragmipedium besseae* • *Rhyncholaeliocattleya* St. Helier • *Stanhopea graveolens*
WARM GROWING *Ludisia discolor* • *Phalaenopsis schilleriana*

Dendrobium victoriae-reginae comes from cool, elevated sites in the Philippines.

Calypso bulbosa is a species in forests and bogs in the US, Europe, and Asia.

Cymbidium tracyanum grows in the mountain forests of China and Thailand.

Paphiopedilum gratrixianum is native to the cloud forests of Laos and Vietnam.

SUMMER

A wide range of orchids flower in summer. To ensure the flowers last well on the plant, screen them from direct sunlight during this period (see p.34).

COOL GROWING *Anguloa clowesii* • *Bletilla:* ochracea; striata • *Brassia:* Orange Delight; Rex • *Calanthe striata* • *Calypso bulbosa* • *Cattleya:* Chic Bonnet; bicolor; luteola; warscewiczii • *Cattlianthe* Hazel Boyd 'Apricot Glow' • *Coelogyne flaccida* • *Cymbidium:* devonianum; erythrostylum • *Dendrobium:* Berry 'Oda'; Spring Dream 'Apollon' • *Dracula bella* • *Guarianthe aurantiaca* • *Lycaste:* aromatica; cruenta; deppei • *Masdevallia:* barleana; infracta; wagneriana • *Maxillaria praestans* • *Miltoniopsis:* Anjou 'St Patrick'; Herrealexandre; Hougemont; Pink Cadillac • *Oncidium:* Jungle Monarch; lanceanum • *Thunia gattonensis*
INTERMEDIATE GROWING *Brassavola nodosa* • *Bulbophyllum:* careyanum; lobbii; macranthum • *Cattleya leopoldii* • *Coelogyne mooreana* 'Westonbirt' • *Dendrobium macrophyllum* • *Epidendrum:* difforme; Plastic Doll • *Miltonia spectabilis* • *Paphiopedilum:* armeniacum; Maudiae 'Coloratum'; niveum; rothschildianum; Vanda M. Pearman • *Stanhopea graveolens*

FALL

Fall-flowering orchids need regular watering during the warmer summer months to ensure that their roots never dry out completely, otherwise the flower buds may be shed prematurely.

COOL GROWING *Cattleya:* bicolor; labiata; luteola • *Cymbidium:* canaliculatum; elegans; tracyanum • *Guarianthe bowringiana* • *Masdevallia:* barleana; wagneriana • *Oncidium:* cheirophorum; lanceanum • *Paphiopedilum fairrieanum* • *Rossioglossum:* grande; 'Rawdon Jester'
INTERMEDIATE GROWING *Aspasia lunata* • *Bulbophyllum macranthum* • *Dendrobium:* Sa-Nook Blue Happiness; Sa-Nook Purple Happiness • *Epidendrum* Plastic Doll • *Miltonia clowesii* • *Paphiopedilum:* concolor; gratrixianum • *Prosthechea radiata*

WINTER

Winter-flowering orchids are highly prized. Temperature and light levels should not drop too low, and watering is critical to ensure that their roots never dry out completely.

COOL GROWING *Cattleya:* maxima; trianae • *Coelogyne:* cristata; flaccida • *Cymbidium:* canaliculatum; Castle of Mey 'Pinkie'; elegans; hookerianum; Kings Lock 'Cooksbridge'; Mighty Remus; Pontac 'Mont Millais'; Portelet Bay; Rosanette; Showgirl; Strathbraan; Strathden 'Cooksbridge Noel' • *Dendrobium:* Spiral Gem 'Universal Topaz'; williamsonii • *Dracula bella* • *Guarianthe bowringiana* • *Laelia:* anceps; autumnalis • *Masdevallia tovarensis* • *Maxillaria porphyrostele* • *Oncidium:* alexandrae; cheirophorum; Jungle Monarch • *Paphiopedilum venustum* • *Pleurothallis restrepioides* • *Rossioglossum:* grande; 'Rawdon Jester'
INTERMEDIATE GROWING *Bulbophyllum ambrosia* • *Dendrobium:* 'Polar Fire'; polysema; Sa-Nook Blue Happiness; Sa-Nook Purple Happiness • *Dendrochilum glumaceum* • *Paphiopedilum:* appletonianum; gratrixianum; The Earl; villosum • *Prosthechea radiata*
WARM GROWING *Angraecum sesquipedale* • *Phalaenopsis:* schilleriana; stuartiana

Cymbidium orchids are among the most rewarding, producing inflorescences heavy with flowers. They are also easy to grow, preferring cooler winter conditions than some other species.

CHOOSING AND BUYING ORCHIDS

Once the province of specialized growers, orchids have become more available and affordable, and consequently popular as house plants. Remarkably versatile, they can be displayed in a variety of ways—in pots, on windowsills, suspended in hanging baskets, or attached to pieces of bark so their flowers are presented at eye level. They can also make a striking contribution to any floral design. There is no shortage of places to visit to find further inspiration to develop your interest in, and increase your knowledge of, these plants.

FINDING INSPIRATION

While shelves of orchids in a supermarket are eye-catching and displays of plants in a garden center may be even more tempting, these outlets usually sell only tried and tested orchids that are readily available from wholesalers. Once you have started an orchid collection, it is worth seeking inspiration in the work of other amateur and professional growers. This will introduce you to rare and wonderful new plants and creative ways to display them. There are plenty of opportunities—start with your local botanic garden, visit an orchid show, or look up orchid societies in your area.

BOTANIC GARDENS AND ORCHID SHOWS

The most accessible place to view a collection of orchids is probably your local botanic garden. These institutions may have hundreds of orchid species and hybrids in their collections, and are often the centers of orchid breeding programs. When visiting, don't forget to look upward in the greenhouse—there may well be plants growing epiphytically on trees, just as they would in the wild. Many gardens attempt to replicate a natural growing environment, for example adding rocks and streams that raise the humidity level, and other plants associated with orchid habitats. Botanic gardens may also host temporary shows, when their collections are supplemented by orchids loaned by other growers or institutions, and sometimes sponsored by governments or large corporations. The biggest orchid show in the world is probably the Japan Grand Prix International Orchid and Flower Show, held in Tokyo, where over a million plants are used to create spectacular exhibits.

This orchid exhibition in Thailand has staged a "natural" orchid landscape featuring rocks and running water.

Flower shows organized by large horticultural organizations can attract exhibitors from around the world.

SOCIETIES, NURSERIES, AND PUBLICATIONS

Organized at local, regional, or national levels, orchid societies are great places to meet fellow enthusiasts, swap plants, and exchange orchid wisdom. They also stage orchid shows where you can view the collections of other growers and even display your own plants.

Make sure to get on the mailing lists of the larger orchid nurseries; many of them host annual open days when their displays are more lavish than usual. These businesses may also offer lectures, demonstrations, and hands-on workshops where you can learn how to care for and propagate orchids directly from professionals, share your experiences of growing orchids, and buy a few more plants.

Look, too, for large plant fairs; these events will often include stands for orchid specialists or floral designers who use orchids in their displays.

JOURNALS AND WEBSITES General gardening magazines occasionally carry features on orchids, but for expert advice and opinions you should look to the journals and newsletters of specialized orchid and horticultural societies. In the UK, for example, *The Orchid Review,* published by The Royal Horticultural Society (RHS), is the oldest continuous publication on orchids, and contains articles on cultivation, classification, plant profiles, and orchid exploration, with all the latest news from the world of orchid growing and showing.

You will, of course, find plenty of orchid information on the internet, but don't take all the advice you find there at face value. Content is based on the author's individual experience of growing orchids under their local conditions. An author living in Florida, for example, may be able to grow species outdoors that could never survive in a more northerly climate.

BUYING ORCHIDS

Orchids are available year-round from a variety of outlets. You will find them for sale at supermarkets, especially around significant dates such as Valentine's Day and Mother's Day. These orchids are likely to be mass-produced phalaenopsis, cymbidiums, or dendrobiums, because these are the easiest to grow and have a long flowering period. Many hybrids have been bred as house plants and their popularity with florists has ensured a wide color range. It is worth visiting a specialized nursery if you are interested in growing more unusual orchids, while online dealers provide the largest selection of all.

WHERE TO BUY ORCHIDS

Orchids in flower are sold by florists, supermarkets, and DIY stores, and many people start their orchid journey with a phalaenopsis (moth orchid) bought from such a store for no more than the price of a bunch of flowers. However, if you are serious about beginning an orchid collection, it is worth visiting a larger garden center or, better still, a specialized nursery where you can seek advice from knowledgeable staff and select from a wider range of plants that have been raised under good conditions. These nurseries sell plants at all price points—from large, mature specimens to young plants that have yet to flower, so you are sure to find something to suit your taste and your budget. What's more, many nurseries also sell plants online (see *right*) and conduct workshops where you can learn the basics of orchid care and get reliable answers to your questions.

Buy plants when they are in flower wherever possible—you'll have no surprises when it comes to the color and shape of the blooms.

CHOOSING A PLANT

If you are buying an orchid in flower it is easy to pick out a healthy plant. Look for bright green leaves (a little yellowing on lower leaves is acceptable) and intact blooms held on a healthy flower stem that doesn't droop under their weight. Choose a plant with plenty of buds so new flowers will follow soon. Check that the roots are healthy, too: this is simple for epiphytic orchids (see p.11) because they are usually sold in transparent pots. The roots should appear firm and pale green/gray in color, never brown and mushy. Transport the orchids carefully, keeping them upright at all times.

Take time to inspect the roots and leaves before purchase.

BUYING ONLINE

Rarer orchids, not normally available in retail outlets, can often be purchased online. Many reputable nurseries sell in this way, packaging plants extremely well to minimize the risk of damage in transit. When your plant arrives, remove it from all its packaging within 24 hours and cut off any damaged tissue. You may find that flower stems have become twisted in transit. Stand the plant in a cool, lightly shaded spot for a day or so, and the stems will straighten up.

You may also find dealers selling small seedlings that are yet to flower at a much lower cost than mature plants. These plants can be good value but the grower may not be able to predict what color their flowers will be—you will need to grow them on for one or two years before they reach flowering size.

Orchid prices vary considerably; good flowering specimens produced by specialized nurseries can be expensive. The cost will be higher if an orchid is rare, stocks are low, or if it is slow or difficult to propagate.

Ansellia africana is just one of many orchid species at risk of extinction through over-collection.

REPUTABLE DEALERS

Trade in wild orchids is highly restricted by international treaty, and only legally propagated plants can be sold. Unfortunately, plants are still collected from the wild and find their way into commerce, usually via the internet. Always buy from reputable traders, who will have propagated the plants themselves or acquired them from a reliable source.

Young seedlings that have yet to reach flowering age provide excellent value, but are somewhat of a gamble.

ORCHIDS IN THE HOME

With enchanting, long-lasting flowers and lush, glossy leaves, orchids make excellent house plants. Most cope well with the demands of life indoors, and some have been bred specially to thrive in home environments. Many orchids are epiphytes (*see p.11*), which can be grown in pots or displayed in less conventional ways, grown attached to bark or in a basket. They do best when conditions in your home mirror those of their natural habitats, with partial shade, consistent warm temperatures, and relatively high humidity.

When growing orchids in groups, check that they all enjoy a similar set of environmental conditions.

POSITION IN THE HOME

Orchids grow well indoors provided that they have enough light, warmth, and humidity. Place your orchids where they get light all day but are not exposed to prolonged direct sunlight; a west- or east-facing aspect is ideal. If light levels are too low, the plants will struggle to grow healthily and fail to flower. As a general rule, keep growing conditions as stable as possible. This may mean that you have to move the plants from one side of a windowsill to the other during hot summer weather or cover the glass with a translucent blind. Orchids love consistent temperatures—around 60–70°F (16–22°C) works well for most—so keep them in a warm room well away from drafts and heaters or vents. Central heating tends to dry the air, but orchids prefer humidities of 50–70 percent. You can raise the humidity by placing a tray of water under the orchid's pot, using pebbles or absorbent clay pellets to raise the pot base above water level.

BASKETS AND BARK

Hanging baskets, usually made of slatted wood, are ideal for growing orchids with trailing stems. They can be suspended from greenhouse or conservatory rafters. In time, the roots will protrude between the slats. Use a coarse grade of potting mix to ensure that none is washed away through the gaps during watering.

Some smaller epiphytes will grow well attached to a piece of bark, secured with a length of fishing line. The bark pieces can be fixed to a conservatory wall or suspended from the ceiling. Mist plants daily in summer, adding fertilizer to the misting water. You can also periodically dunk the whole plant in a bucket of water and allow to drain before reattaching. You can divide the orchid (see p.43) and attach daughter plants to fresh pieces of bark.

A piece of bark provides support for this epiphytic orchid.

Slatted wood hanging baskets bring orchid displays to head height.

This moth orchid grows in a clear plastic pot set within a cache pot. It sits on moistened clay pellets that help to increase local humidity (see p.37).

ORCHIDS IN POTS

Some orchids are terrestrial, growing with their roots in the ground, while others are epiphytes that grow with their roots exposed to light, rain, and air (see p.11–12). Terrestrial orchids can be grown outdoors if the climate is suitable, or in indoors in terra-cotta, plastic, or stoneware pots filled with terrestrial orchid potting mix (see p.41).

Epiphytic orchids are usually sold and grown in clear plastic pots that allow light to reach their roots. The pots contain epiphytic orchid potting mix (see p.11–12). You can disguise the plastic pots by placing them into decorative cache pots, which will also provide some ballast. Ensure that the surface roots can grow freely. All pots must have drainage holes in their bases so the plant never sits in water.

Some orchids, notably vandas, are sold in clay pots that have holes in the sides that allow roots to grow through them and which hold little more than a handful of potting mix.

A terrarium can contain a mixture of plants to provide floral and foliar interest throughout the year.

TERRARIUMS

Individual or grouped orchids can be displayed to great effect in a glass tank, or terrarium. This has the advantage of screening plants from drafts and slightly raises the humidity around them. A clean fish or reptile tank works perfectly. The tank can be left open, or—to raise the humidity further—fitted with a lid. Position your terrarium in a bright position but out of direct sunlight.

WARDIAN CASES

An elegant and traditional way to display orchids is in a Wardian case. Such enclosures were used by the plant hunters who first collected orchids from the wild and bought them home on sea journeys that often lasted many weeks. They are named after the English plant collector Nathaniel Bagshaw Ward (1791–1868).

Plants often perished in transit from exposure to rough weather until the invention of the Wardian case.

ORCHIDS AND FLORAL DESIGN

The use of orchids in floral design has expanded hugely in recent years, and they are now in the top ten most popular cut flowers. Perhaps unexpectedly, orchid blooms in a vase of water can last longer than they do when on the plant—often for several weeks—outliving many other popular cut flowers. Blooms produced under glass for the floristry trade are pristine but are usually scentless (to appeal to the widest market). You can cut flowers from your own plants and arrange them in vases—a great way to enjoy blooms that you have raised in a greenhouse (see pp.30–31).

Dendrobium flowers may last one week after cutting, but some cymbidiums (pictured) and oncidiums will still look good after three weeks.

ORCHIDS AS CUT FLOWERS

Orchids with large, colorful, and robust long-stemmed flowers are the best choices for cutting and display. Paphiopedilums, oncidiums, and vandas are all available in the cut flower trade, but the most common are cattleyas, the classic choice for corsages and buttonholes; phalaenopsis, which have beautifully colored and patterned petals; dendrobiums, which have very resilient and colorful flowers; and cymbidiums, which have usefully long stems and wilt-resistant blooms.

Orchids do not always integrate well with other cut flowers and are displayed to best effect as singletons in tall, narrow vases, giving the showy, exotic flowers space to impress.

To cut a flower or flower stem from one of your plants, wait until the blooms are fully open. Use a sharp knife to sever the flower stem at its base, retaining as much length as possible. Stand the stem in tepid water in a vase and add flower food, which will extend the life of the flower. Leave in a cool, shaded place overnight before moving the vase into its display position. Avoid placing cut flowers near your fruit bowl as gases given off by ripening fruit will make the flowers age more rapidly. Top up the water regularly. Stems of airy foliage, such as asparagus fern, can be added to complement the flowers.

Orchid displays, such as this arrangement of inflorescences in tall glass vases, are a testament to the creativity of florists and designers.

With their elegant flowers, vandas make a big impact in this table decoration for a wedding.

IKEBANA

Orchids often feature in ikebana, a traditional Japanese art that focuses on movement, balance, and harmony in design. An ikebana arrangement is typically small in scale, emphasizes fine lines, and, through a "less is more" approach, reveals the subtle beauty of the flowers through contrast with other natural materials.

The tradition of ikebana dates back over one thousand years.

PROFESSIONAL DISPLAYS

Orchids rival roses as the go-to flowers for wedding floristry because—despite their elegant appearance—they are quite robust and easy to transport. They can be used for bridal bouquets, corsages, and buttonholes, as well as for table centerpieces at the wedding breakfast.

Professional florists often use flower tubes, made of clear plastic or glass, that hold an individual flower stem. These can then be mounted to create a large display, such as one you might see at a wedding, in a luxury hotel's reception area, or at a glamorous corporate event. Such displays are expensive to create but extremely impactful.

ORCHIDS UNDER GLASS

Many orchids will grow happily on a windowsill indoors, but some are far better suited to a greenhouse or conservatory. Orchids grown in baskets, for example, are easier to water if there is a tiled or brick floor below onto which water can drain, and plants grown attached to bark slabs need frequent misting, which is more practical in such a location. Some orchids require consistently high temperature or humidity, which is easier to achieve under glass. You can bring greenhouse plants indoors for a short period while they are in bloom before returning them to their usual quarters.

HEATED GREENHOUSES

You can grow orchids in a heated greenhouse on their own or alongside other plants. Adequate temperatures can be maintained in spring and fall using gas or electric heaters fitted with thermostats, but additional insulation, such as double glazing or bubble wrap stretched over the glass, may be needed in winter.

To satisfy the widest range of plants, aim for an intermediate range (see p.34), no lower than 55°F (13°C) in winter and no higher than 75°F (24°C) in summer.

Most cool and warm growing types will tolerate these conditions; heat-loving tropical orchids grown in baskets and on bark can be hung from the rafters at the top of the greenhouse where it is a few degrees warmer. To avoid scorch in summer, use fine netting to screen the plants; keep the greenhouse ventilated, and hose down the floor twice a day with water to lower the temperature.

If you have a large greenhouse, you can hang thick plastic curtains to divide it into separate sections for orchids with differing temperature requirements; heat each area accordingly.

Prevent the temperature in your greenhouse from rising too high in summer by opening vents in the daytime.

UNHEATED GREENHOUSES

An unheated greenhouse or alpine house is ideal for orchids such as pleiones that can withstand a few degrees of winter frost. While these and some others can tolerate low temperatures, they hate to have wet roots, so make sure not to overwater; ventilate the plants well, even in winter, to prevent a buildup of stagnant air.

In summer, pleiones can easily overheat, so make sure to open greenhouse vents and doors in the daytime or move the plants to a sheltered, shaded place outdoors. A cool greenhouse can also be a suitable place to rest orchids in spring and fall after they have flowered.

A heated greenhouse will greatly increase the range of orchids that you can grow successfully.

CONSERVATORIES

Tropical orchids are best grown in a conservatory, where their needs for consistently warm temperatures and humidity are easiest to meet, especially in winter. Guard against excessive heat and light levels in summer—put up shades on the windows and hose down the floor twice daily to keep plants cool and raise humidity.

Good ventilation and frequent misting can also help regulate the temperature, though if you want to use the conservatory as a space for relaxation in summer, it can be more practical to move the plants outdoors as long as nighttime temperatures do not drop too low (see p.34).

TRACKING THE TEMPERATURE

To be certain you are maintaining the optimum temperature for your plants, invest in a minimum–maximum thermometer that records and displays the two extremes of temperature. These are usually wall mounted. Sophisticated digital models have features that allow you to monitor the temperature remotely.

Digital thermometers can track temperature fluctuations over days and weeks.

TOP TIP WHEN MOVING FLOWERING PLANTS INTO A LIVING ROOM FOR DISPLAY, WAIT UNTIL THE FLOWERS ARE ALMOST FULLY OPEN TO AVOID THE RISK OF PREMATURE BUD DROP.

Growing orchids in your conservatory will enhance your enjoyment of the space.

Orchids need repotting when they begin to grow out of their containers or when their chunky potting mix starts to decay and break down into small pieces.

CARE AND MAINTENANCE

Orchids are generally resilient and less prone to problems than many other house plants, but do need appropriate care if they are to thrive. Finding the right position, where their needs for light and warmth are met, is half the battle. Then it is simply a matter of giving them enough water and fertilizer at the right time to ensure they continue to flourish. Regular inspection of your plants is key to keeping them happy, healthy, and producing quantities of beautiful flowers.

TEMPERATURE AND LIGHT

Providing your orchids with appropriate temperature and light levels is a key aspect of successful cultivation. Many orchids will be perfectly happy growing near a window in a typical centrally heated home, but warm growing types are better suited to a heated conservatory (see p.30). Some species can tolerate short periods at temperatures lower than the recommended winter minimum but prolonged cold will lead to leaf loss and eventual death. The few orchids that can survive below freezing, such as pleiones, are best grown in an unheated greenhouse or conservatory.

Phalaenopsis are warm-growing orchids from the tropics.

LIGHT LEVELS

The majority of orchids are tropical or subtropical plants that are used to growing under conditions of day length, light, and temperature that remain fairly constant throughout the year. In the temperate zones of Europe and the US, these conditions can fluctuate considerably; winter days are short, dull, and cold, while summer days are longer than in the tropics and brighter than in the natural forest habitats of many orchids. Try to replicate the original growing conditions by keeping orchids slightly shaded in summer, topping up light levels in the winter, and ensuring that plants are kept in temperatures appropriate to their needs (see below).

NEED TO KNOW
The temperature requirements of orchids vary even within genera. Plants are usually categorized as below, the temperature range indicating the winter minimum and the summer maximum:
- Cool growing: 50–68°F (10–20°C)
- Intermediate growing: 54–74°F (12–22°C)
- Warm growing: 59–77°F (15–25°C)

TOP TIP SCREEN ORCHIDS GROWING ON A WINDOW SILL WITH A SHEER BLIND OR A NET ACROSS THE GLASS. ALTERNATIVELY, MOVE THEM TO ONE SIDE OF THE WINDOW SO THE LIGHT IS ON THEM IS INDIRECT.

Modern LED growing lamps run cold so they are safe to leave on while consuming little power.

USING A GROWING LAMP

Growing lamps simulate natural light. They are commonly used by gardeners to help in the germination of seedlings, but can also perk up orchids in winter and help promote flowering in plants that produce their blooms in winter (because flower buds that develop in the fall may fail to open without adequate light). Growing lamps contain LEDs that emit blue light (for leafy growth) and red (for flower production); the light is cold, so you need not worry about burning the leaves. Position the lamps so light falls evenly over the plants and set their timers so they turn on for a few hours to overlap with the fading natural light.

"RESTING" AN ORCHID

In tropical and subtropical habitats, orchids are often in growth year-round. In our homes, where there is not enough light to keep them active in winter, you can induce a period of dormancy in which the orchid rests for six to eight weeks. To do this, keep orchids cool and water just enough to keep the potting mix barely moist. This will slow down or pause growth. As the days begin to lengthen, just after the winter solstice, start watering more freely and begin feeding. Orchids can also be rested after a long period of flowering, which can exhaust the plant.

Cool growing species, such as this *Dendrochilum uncatum*, will benefit from resting over winter.

SUMMERING OUTDOORS

If possible, move your orchids outdoors in the summer months. There, beneficial insects will feed on any pests that may be present on the plants, and exposure to rainwater and the free movement of air will help firm up growth.

Place the plants in a sheltered, shady area, protected from strong winds and hot sunshine. Orchids growing on bark rafts or in baskets can be hung from tree branches. Watch out for slugs. Many orchids have leaves that are too tough to appeal to these pests, but some may need to be protected.

Moving orchids outdoors during warm weather can improve their health.

WATERING AND FEEDING

All plants need water to survive and grow. In their wild habitats, orchids are often found in damp, humid environments that keep them permanently moist. In the home, however, they need regular applications of water, because the potting mix in which they are grown is extremely free draining. Orchid roots are also often exposed to the air, so they are more prone to drying out than those of other plants. While orchids do not require intensive feeding, regular applications of a well-diluted fertilizer are important if they are to grow strongly and flower prolifically.

HOW TO WATER

The aim of watering is to keep your orchid's roots moist but never standing in liquid; waterlogging will quickly kill a plant. Water orchids freely when they are growing strongly, usually in spring and summer, and reduce the amount and frequency in winter or if resting the orchid after flowering (see p.35). If your plant is growing in a transparent pot, you can easily check its water status.

Always pour the water close to the surface around the base of the plant to avoid soaking the pseudobulbs where moisture can collect and cause rot. If you have a lot of orchids, it may be easier to stand all your plants in a sink filled with water to the depth of the pots for 10 minutes, then let the plants drain.

KNOW YOUR WATER SUPPLY If possible, use fresh rain water for your orchids—it is well oxygenated and free of chemicals, such as chlorine. Avoid stored rain water, which may harbor microbes. Tap water is usually fine to use, with a few provisos. Depending on its source, tap water may be soft or hard (containing dissolved calcium salts that cause scale to build up on hot water pipes). Hard water is not good for orchids, but it can be improved a little by boiling it and allowing it to cool before watering. Do not use water that has been treated in a water softener as it is likely to contain excess sodium salt.

Water the potting mix rather than the plant so that water does not collect in the leaf bases.

Pseudobulbs store water and nutrients. A water-stressed plant may display puckered pseudobulbs, as seen here.

WATER STORAGE AND WINTER WATERING

Some orchids have pseudobulbs (see p.14) that store water and make it available to the plant when it is dormant (usually in the winter). Orchids that lack pseudobulbs, such as phalaenopsis, have thickened leaves that perform a similar water-storage function. Plump, firm pseudobulbs (or leaves in orchids that lack pseudobulbs) indicate that a plant has an adequate stored supply; wrinkled pseudobulbs (or puckered, dull leaves) indicate that winter watering is needed. While you can rely on these signs, few orchids should be allowed to dry out in winter, so water occasionally to ensure they never become completely dry.

Regular misting raises the humidity level around orchids and also helps keep them cool.

HUMIDITY

Many orchids are rain- or cloud-forest plants used to growing in a damp, humid environment. It isn't practical to replicate these conditions in the home, but you can raise humidity around plants by one of the following methods.

- Mist the plants once or twice daily with a fine spray. Misting lowers the temperature around the plants, so may not be necessary in winter.

- Stand plants on trays filled with a layer of clay pellets (available from orchid suppliers and larger garden centers). Keep the pellets moist: water evaporates from them, creating a pocket of humidity around the orchids.
- Group orchids together; this establishes a humid microclimate in which water evaporates more slowly.
- Place plants in a terrarium (see p.27), which raises local humidity; this is suitable for small orchids only.

FEEDING

Like all plants, orchids need a balance of mineral nutrients to grow well. However, their requirements are very low, making general garden fertilizer too rich for use with orchids. Instead, choose a dedicated orchid fertilizer, which can be bought from a garden center or online. There are two types: high-nitrogen fertilizers should be applied in spring or after a period of dormancy; high-potassium foods are usually applied in summer to promote flowering and firm up the growth, which will help the plant survive low temperatures over winter.

Most orchid fertilizers are sold in liquid form. Dilute as instructed and water into the potting mix. Some are sprays which should be applied directly over the leaves. Do not overfeed your orchids—the resulting lush growth is more susceptible to disease.

Orchid fertilizers are sometimes sold in phials that can be inserted directly into the potting mix for gradual release of food.

ORCHIDS IN FLOWER

With the single exception of *Ludisia discolor (see p.99)*, orchids are cultivated for their flowers. Since they are grown under cover, the flowers are usually perfect, unlike the blooms of garden plants that routinely fall victim to wind, heavy rainfall, hail, or pest attack. They are also long-lived, remaining on the plant for weeks. Don't be afraid of moving plants when they are in flower to a position in the home where you can enjoy them to the fullest, even if the light and temperature may be less than ideal.

Many orchid flowers grow atop long stems and will need to be tied to a stake for support.

DEADHEADING

Remove orchid flowers as they fade—the old flowers are unsightly and may attract fungi that can affect the whole plant. If the flowers are carried singly, cut back the whole stem to the base. A few orchids can reflower from the same stem; in such cases, just cut off the flower where it meets the stem. If the flowers are produced in clusters, remove individual flowers within the cluster, then, when they have all faded, cut back the whole stem.

Check your orchids regularly and pinch or cut off dead flowers promptly to help maintain plant health.

GETTING A PHALAENOPSIS TO REFLOWER

When all the flowers have faded on your phalaenopsis, do not cut back the whole stem. Instead, shorten it, cutting just above a node below the flower cluster. These nodes resemble tiny leaves to one side of the stem. A new shoot carrying more flowers will grow from the node. If you do this consistently, and keep feeding the plant, it should flower for several months.

When all the flowers in your phalaenopsis's inflorescence have faded, it is time to shorten the stem.

Look closely at the phalaenopsis stem to identify a suitable node above which the stem can be cut.

Pleione orchids typically have small shoots and proportionally large, low flowers, making them resemble crocuses in growth habit.

STAKING ORCHIDS

Orchids carry their flowers in different ways. Some, such as pleiones, produce flowers on short stems, so the blooms nestle among the leaves. Stanhopeas and others have long, trailing stems that naturally hang downward, with the flowers at the stem tips, so are best displayed in baskets. However, many orchids have tall, upright stems and carry their flowers well above the foliage. The stems are often very slender, and the weight of the flowers can cause them to lean over and even break, so they benefit from support. Similarly, naturally arching stems can be staked to hold them more upright, which may be desirable in a confined space.

Thin wooden, bamboo, or plastic canes can be used to support stems. As soon as you see a flowering stem appear, push a cane into the potting mix about ½ in (1 cm) away from the stem base. This is easiest to do if the potting mix is fairly dry. Taking care not to damage the root system, push the cane right to the bottom of the pot so it is securely anchored in position. Attach the stem to the cane as it grows, either using clips available from orchid suppliers or with short lengths of string. Do not use wire or make the ties too tight—this could damage the stem.

TOP TIP TO AVOID EYE INJURIES, COVER THE UPPER END OF A CANE USED TO SUPPORT A STEM WITH A PLASTIC CAP OR SMALL BALL OF MODELING CLAY.

The flowers of Stanhopea jenischiana hang downward to mimic and attract their pollinators—Euglossine bees.

REPOTTING AN ORCHID

Healthy orchids usually outgrow their containers in a couple of years and require repotting. Moving them into larger containers provides the space needed for continued growth and flowering and refreshes the potting mix, which will deteriorate and even rot over time.

Repotting is the ideal time to examine your plant and identify and cut out older, unproductive parts of the top growth and root system. Without repotting, plants will become congested, flowering will be inhibited, and their overall health may suffer. For large, impressive plants, repot regularly.

HOW TO REPOT

The time to repot an orchid is when it has visibly filled its pot and begun to "flow" over the sides. Repot in early spring, when new growth is beginning, or after flowering. The new pot should be larger but not too big—the roots need to wrap quickly around the fresh potting mix. Water the plant and allow it to drain completely before repotting. This makes it easier to remove it from the pot.

YOU WILL NEED Pot • broken crocks or recycled polystyrene packaging • orchid potting mix • scissors or pruners

1 Place broken terra-cotta pieces or chunks of polystyrene in the bottom of the new pot to aid drainage, and top with a layer of fresh potting mix. Remove the orchid from its old pot. Shake or pull off all the old soil. Take care not to damage the roots.
2 Cut off any old, dead roots with scissors or pruners. Trim back longer roots so they fit easily in the new pot. Cut off any old, withered pseudobulbs.
3 Place the orchid in the new pot. For orchids without pseudobulbs (such as phalaenopsis), position the plant centrally. For orchids with pseudobulbs, set the oldest pseudobulb against the rim of the pot, so the newer ones on the other side of the plant can to grow into fresh potting mix.

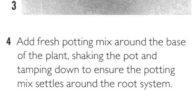

4 Add fresh potting mix around the base of the plant, shaking the pot and tamping down to ensure the potting mix settles around the root system.

Water the plant well to consolidate the potting mix around the roots. Fresh potting mix can dry out quickly, so water again over the next few days.

ORCHID MEDIA

Orchid growing media are different from those used for other plants. Conventional potting mixes are weighty and moisture-retentive, whereas orchid media have a much more open texture and are designed to imitate the plant litter in which orchids are frequently found in the wild.

Standard orchid potting mix comprises coarse bark chips, the main function of which is to support the root system and anchor the plant in its pot. It typically contains no additional nutrients, but as the chips break down, low levels of nutrients become available to the plant via its root system. This potting mix is suitable for nearly all epiphytic orchids (it is often called "epiphytic orchid medium") and many terrestrial orchids.

Potting mix formulated for terrestrial orchids is based on a finer grade of bark and is more soil-like in its composition than epiphytic orchid potting mix. It is often recommended for orchids with fine root systems.

Sphagnum moss can be used as an additive to orchid potting mix because it holds water well while also allowing good drainage.

Epiphytic orchid potting mix contains bark chips that ensure good drainage.

Terrestrial orchid potting mix is finer and retains moisture around the roots.

POTTING MIX ADDITIVES

Some terrestrial orchids appreciate a reliably damp potting mix around their roots. Certain materials can be added to terrestrial potting mix to improve moisture retention, while also maintaining the good drainage that is critical for all orchids.

Sphagnum moss Packed around orchid roots, this naturally occurring material helps with moisture retention.
Coir A natural fiber extracted from the husk of coconut, this is a byproduct of the coconut industry and can be substituted for sphagnum moss.
Rockwool This substance, which is also used as an insulating material in house building, is another alternative to sphagnum moss.

Perlite This lightweight, granular material looks and feels like crushed polystyrene but is actually made from expanded volcanic glass. It is extremely porous, so can absorb water when added to media while also improving drainage.
Vermiculite This is a naturally occurring, lightweight, sand-colored mineral with similar properties to perlite. It helps aerate media while also retaining moisture.

TOP TIP PERLITE AND VERMICULITE ARE DUSTY MATERIALS THAT CAN THROW UP A CLOUD OF TINY, POTENTIALLY IRRITANT, PARTICLES WHEN YOU OPEN THE BAG. MOISTEN THEM IN THE BAG WITH A LITTLE WATER ON OPENING OR WEAR A FACE MASK WHEN HANDLING.

PROPAGATING ORCHIDS

If you'd like to increase your stock of plants or produce an orchid for sale or to give to a friend, you can try propagating from an existing plant. Growing orchids from seed is very difficult, but it is simple to split certain plants into two or more parts. Dividing an orchid brings other benefits.

It refreshes a plant, stimulating new growth, and in the process you can discard older parts that are vulnerable to disease. Orchids can be divided at any time, except when flowering, but it is best to divide in spring, when new growth is beginning and the active parts of the plant are most easily identified.

TECHNIQUES

Unlike many plants, orchids are hard to grow from seed. They need specific pollinators (see p.16), usually absent in their new homes, and even if they do set seed, this is dustlike and difficult to handle. Orchid seeds contain no nutrients to nourish the embryo plants and rely on associations called mycorrhizae that they form with fungi in the soil. Professional orchid breeders germinate seeds on special gels containing growth hormones and nutrients: this is a process that requires specialized knowledge and equipment.

Fortunately, several techniques can be used to propagate orchids vegetatively (without the production of seed), but not all techniques are suitable for all types of orchid. The common technique of division can be used for most sympodial orchids (those with pseudobulbs) and is described opposite.

Other propagation techniques include growing new plants from the back bulbs of sympodial orchids (see p.14), or from tiny plants called keikis (see p.44) that may form on the stems of orchids such as phalaenopsis and dendrobiums.

Growing orchids from seed requires laboratory conditions that would be extremely difficult to replicate at home.

DIVIDING
SYMPODIAL ORCHIDS

To divide a sympodial orchid, use a clean, sharp knife or pruners to make your cuts. Dormant back bulbs (see p.14) can be included in the divisions because they help feed the new growth. Alternatively, they can be removed for growing on separately (see p.44).

YOU WILL NEED Sharp knife • pruners • pots • broken crocks or recycled polystyrene • orchid potting mix

1 Remove the parent plant from its pot and clean away all the old potting mix from around the roots. Pull away any dead leaves that may still be attached to the pseudobulbs.

2 Cut off any obviously dead roots and shorten any overlong ones.

3 Turning the plant in your hands, assess where best to make the cuts. If you want plants that will flower the next year, each division should have at least three active growing points (that is three pseudobulbs carrying green, healthy leaves). Smaller divisions will take a couple of years to reach flowering size.

4 Depending on the type of orchid, you may be able to divide it using only your hands; if not, use a knife to help tease the sections apart. If the orchid has a thick rhizome, cut through it with a sharp knife or pruners.

5 Line the new pots with broken crocks or polystyrene chips to improve drainage and top off with a layer of orchid potting mix. Set each division with its oldest pseudobulb against the rim of the pot, so the plant can grow out on the other side to fill the container.

6 Feed fresh potting mix around the roots. Shake the pot so the potting mix settles and firm it down. Water the plants well; keep watering over the next few days because fresh orchid mix is prone to drying out.

TOP TIP POT UP THE DIVISIONS INTO POTS WITH ENOUGH ROOM FOR TWO OR THREE YEARS' GROWTH.

BACK BULBS, KEIKIS, AND CUTTINGS

Simple division is the most straightforward and widespread means of propagating sympodial orchids (see pp.42–43). However, other methods are available. Dormant back bulbs can be separated from an orchid and induced to grow into new plants; and keikis—baby plants—can be separated from stems to grow on as individuals. Dendrobiums and similar orchids can be propagated using a technique in which their cane-like pseudobulbs are cut and encouraged to root.

Cut off a back bulb at repotting time and place it under growing conditions that will induce rooting.

BACK BULBS

Back bulbs are older pseudobulbs that no longer produce leaves (see p.14). They can be cut away from a plant along with their roots and used to produce a new orchid. The ideal time to do this is when repotting the orchid. Strip away any old, papery leaves from the base of the back bulb and trim off any dead roots. Wrap the back bulb's root system in damp sphagnum moss, or an alternative (see p.41), and pot in a small container. Place the pot in a heated propagator positioned in indirect light. Mist the moss regularly. New growth should appear around the base of the pseudobulb after around six to eight weeks. When this is well developed, pot the pseudobulb up into standard orchid potting mix.

KEIKIS

Keiki is a Hawaiian word meaning "baby." In the orchid world, a keiki is a complete new little plant that appears on the stems of certain orchids, especially those that have been kept too warm and damp over winter. They are often seen on phalaenopsis and dendrobiums and provide an excellent method of propagating a plant that may otherwise be unsuitable for division.

Keikis look like miniature versions of the parent plant. Wait until they are large enough to handle easily and have a well-developed root system. Carefully detach the keiki from the parent. Either peel it away gently by hand or use a sharp blade, such as a scalpel, to remove it intact. Pot it up into a small pot filled with a fibrous but free-draining orchid potting mix. Move the keiki into a larger pot filled with standard orchid potting mix once it has put on visible growth.

Keikis appear spontaneously on the stems of phalaenopsis and other orchids and provide an easy way to propagate.

Using a sharp blade or scissors, cut the keiki away from its parent plant and pot it in fibrous potting mix.

USING A PROPAGATOR

A propagator is an essential piece of equipment if you want to grow orchids from back bulbs or cuttings. It consists of a shallow plastic tray fitted with an electric heating element in its base and a clear plastic cover that allows in light. Vents in the lid promote good air circulation. Larger propagators are usually fitted with thermostats that allow you to regulate the temperature within. If there is no thermostat, open the vents or remove the lid completely during the day, aiming to keep the temperature as close as possible to 70°F (21°C) around the clock.

Before placing potted pseudobulbs or stem cuttings in the propagator, allow it warm up for an hour or so. Mist the plants daily to keep them moist. Position the propagator in a light place but out of direct sunlight to prevent overheating.

A heated propagator is key to success when growing orchids from back bulbs or cuttings.

PROPAGATING A DENDROBIUM FROM CUTTINGS

Dendrobiums, and other orchids with cane-like pseudobulbs, can be propagated by cutting the canes into short sections, and setting them on shallow trays (such as small seed trays) filled with damp sphagnum moss (or an alternative).

YOU WILL NEED Sharp knife • fungicide power • seed tray • sphagnum moss (or similar) • propagator

1 In spring or summer, remove a cane, severing it near the base of the plant to avoid leaving a stump.
2 Cut the cane into sections around 2 in (5 cm) long. Each section should have at least two nodes, identifiable as scars where leaves have been shed.
3 Treat the cut ends of the sections with a plant fungicide to prevent rotting.
4 Place the cuttings lengthwise on the moss, pressing them down slightly to ensure good adhesion. Put them in a heated propagator out of direct sunlight. In around three months, new growth should appear on the cuttings, and roots should emerge on the underside. At this point, pot up the sections individually in small pots filled with a fine-grade orchid potting mix.

TOP TIP KEEP BACK BULBS GROWING VIGOROUSLY BY REPOTTING THEM EVERY SIX MONTHS UNTIL THEY REACH FLOWERING SIZE; THEN FEED THEM WITH A NITROGEN-RICH FERTILIZER THROUGHOUT SPRING AND SUMMER.

Yellowing of lower parts of leaves
may be the result of water being trapped
in the leaf bases, or of a sudden change in
the plant's environment.

TROUBLESHOOTING

Properly cared for, orchids are largely trouble free. Problems, when they occur, are usually easy to diagnose and solve, and even neglected plants can be brought back from the brink and given a new lease on life. Prevention is always better than cure, so maintaining appropriate growing conditions is key to success. Common sense should prevail; always quarantine new plants before adding them to your main collection; and maintain good hygiene, using sharp, clean tools and clearing organic debris away from plants.

MAINTAINING PLANT HEALTH

Orchids have an undeserved reputation for being temperamental and difficult to care for. In fact, they are susceptible to fewer problems than many other widely grown houseplants. If you do spot an issue, the key advice is to deal with it promptly because curing a seriously affected plant is not always possible. As with all plants, prevention is better than cure because healthy, strong-growing plants are more resistant to pests and diseases than those that are neglected and weak.

Cleaning orchid leaves makes them look and function better. Wipe them with a sponge or absorbent cloth moistened with cooled boiled water to avoid mineral deposits.

PREVENTION CHECKLIST

Use the following checklist to ensure orchids are always at their best.

- Water frequently during the growing period, usually spring–summer, to keep leaves and pseudobulbs firm and healthy. Drain plants fully after watering; excess moisture around the roots can lead to rot and death.
- Feed plants when they are in growth. Use nitrogen-high fertilizers to build leaf area just as new growth begins (usually in spring) then switch to a potassium-rich type to firm up the pseudobulbs and promote flowering. Follow instructions on the fertilizer to avoid overfeeding.
- Maintain appropriate light levels. Screen plants from strong sunlight in summer but expose them to maximum light in winter.
- Protect plants from extremes of heat and cold. Regulate summer temperature by shading, misting, and providing good ventilation. In winter, move plants to a place where the temperature never drops below the recommended minimum.
- Deadhead promptly. Remove faded flowers from the plant before they decay; rotting blooms attract fungi.
- Repot when plants fill their pots. This provides new growing space and lets you remove spent or moldy soil. Assess your plants in the process and cut off any old, withered pseudobulbs that may be prone to disease.

RECOGNIZING AN AILING PLANT

Every time you water your orchid, take a minute to inspect its leaves (not forgetting their undersides), flowers, and roots for signs of problems. These may be caused by pests, diseases, or—more

Dry roots and yellowing leaves point to too little water.

likely—inappropriate growing conditions, which are usually easily remedied. Look to the most likely causes—incorrect light and temperature levels and too much or too little moisture. These are signs of an ailing plant and their possible causes:

- Leaves distorted or pleated: low humidity or too little water
- Yellowing leaves: water in leaf bases or sudden change in environment
- Pseudobulbs feel soft: too much water
- Flower buds form but fail to open: too much or too little water; exposure to hot or cold air
- Roots brown and mushy, or dull and shriveled: too much/too little water

Next, check any symptoms that your plant displays against those of the most common pests and diseases (see pp.50–53). Deal with them promptly.

A predatory mite attacks a two-spotted spider mite.

BIOLOGICAL CONTROLS

Predators of orchid pests can be bought online or by mail order. Releasing these predators is a chemical-free way of controlling pests such as aphids and spider mites. These biological control agents are only effective if released in an enclosed space, such as a greenhouse or conservatory, and should be introduced as soon as the pest is noticed as it will be weeks before the control becomes fully effective.

QUARANTINING AN AILING PLANT

If you suspect that the problem affecting your orchid is caused by a particular pest or disease, it is good practice to isolate that plant from the rest of your collection while you deal with it. Keep it

separate for at least a month after you have treated the problem. When buying new plants, keep them separate for a month, too, just in case they are harboring any transmissible problems.

Place a sick orchid in a room of its own, well away from other plants—bugs can be very mobile.

CHEMICAL CONTROLS

Few reliable pesticides and fungicides are available to today's gardeners. The insecticides are usually based on fatty acids or soaps: they leave no active residues, so need to be reapplied to treat a persistent problem. Fungicides are available to deal with black rot and other fungal diseases; take care when applying them as some products can mark open flowers. Spray over leaves and unopened buds only.

Always apply chemicals following the manufacturer's instructions.

COMMON ORCHID PESTS

Orchids can be affected by a range of insect and other invertebrate pests that also attack other house plants. In an enclosed environment, such as a greenhouse or conservatory, their natural predators will not be present, so pests can proliferate rapidly; many are capable of breeding throughout the year. They are often introduced on new plants, so check these carefully for any signs of pest damage on purchase and isolate if necessary. Most orchid pests are easy to deal with, provided you take action quickly.

APHIDS

HOW TO IDENTIFY These are small, often wingless, soft-bodied, pear-shaped, insects that suck the sap from leaves and stems. Flowers appear mottled and distorted and buds may fail to open. The orchid aphid *Cerataphis lataniae* is often the culprit, but garden aphids may also find their way indoors in summer.
CONTROL Pick off insects or remove them with water spray. Use insecticide for heavier attacks. The biological controls *Aphidoletes aphidimyza* and *Aphidius* spp. may be effective.
PREVENTION Place plants outdoors during the milder months, when their natural predators are active.

Aphids may be a variety of colors including green, yellow, brown, pink, gray, and black.

RED SPIDER MITE

HOW TO IDENTIFY These tiny eight-legged mites are usually identified by the damage they cause. Leaves are marked by fine stippling on the upper side. In severe cases, the leaves turn yellow. The mites' webs may be visible on the undersides.
CONTROL This pest rapidly reproduces and is resistant to many pesticides. In a greenhouse or conservatory, the mite *Phytoseiulus persimilis* may be effective as a biological control.
PREVENTION In greenhouses, avoid high temperatures (in which the pests will proliferate) by maintaining high humidity through frequent spraying and keeping plants shaded.

Discourage mites by misting in summer to increase humidity.

SLUGS

HOW TO IDENTIFY These familiar slimy garden mollusks, often active at night, leave telltale silvery trails on surfaces. They favor cool, damp situations and can cause severe damage, destroying flower buds and stalks, and root tips.
CONTROL Check over your plants at night and pick off the pests by hand. Use slug pellets as a last resort.
PREVENTION Practice good hygiene by clearing away any plant debris from around the base of plants that might shelter the pests.

Slugs are among the most destructive pests outdoors; indoor plants are usually out of their reach.

THRIPS

HOW TO IDENTIFY These tiny yellow or black flies cause silvery flecking on flowers and leaves. Unopened flower buds may be distorted. They commonly attack plants during prolonged periods of dry weather.
CONTROL Spray plants with an approved insecticide, though resistance is widespread. Biological controls, such as *Amblyseius* spp., may be successful.
PREVENTION In greenhouses and conservatories, lower the temperature by watering plants regularly, ventilating well, and using shading.

Thrips cause direct damage but can also carry plant viruses.

SCALE INSECTS

HOW TO IDENTIFY These sap-sucking insects often cluster on stems and the lower surfaces of leaves. The sugary "honeydew" they excrete drips down and attracts sooty molds (see pp.52–53). Growth slows on affected plants.
CONTROL Spray with insecticide (most effective on newly hatched nymphs that have yet to develop their outer coating). The biological control *Metaphycus helvolus* may be effective in a greenhouse or conservatory.
PREVENTION Indoors, scale insects can breed year-round, so check your plants regularly and deal with the pest promptly.

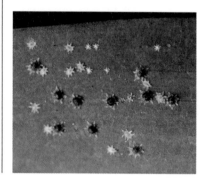

These insects have hard outer shells and are visible to the naked eye. They can be yellow, brown, dark gray, or white.

MEALYBUGS

HOW TO IDENTIFY These bugs tend to live together in clusters in leaf axils and leaf sheaths, occasionally on plant roots. They suck sap and then excrete excess sugars as "honeydew," which drops onto lower parts of the plant and attracts sooty molds (see pp.52–53), giving the surfaces a blackened appearance.
CONTROL Dab bugs with a cotton swab soaked in rubbing alcohol. In a greenhouse or conservatory, introduce the ladybug *Cryptolaemus montrouzieri* as a biological control.
PREVENTION Check any new plants carefully for any signs of the pest and isolate them for at least a month.

Mealybugs are hard to spot because they can be present in the potting mix.

DEALING WITH ANTS

Ants are not orchid pests in themselves, but need to be controlled if your plants are affected by scale insects or mealybugs (see *above and left*). This is because ants are attracted to the honeydew excreted by the orchid pests, which they collect for their young. In the process, they transfer the pests' eggs from plant to plant, thus making the scale insect or mealybug problem much worse. Ant traps are effective in controlling their populations.

Ant traps are widely available and simple to deploy.

COMMON ORCHID DISEASES

The effect of disease is to weaken a plant, with the result that an affected orchid often looks like a neglected one, making a precise diagnosis tricky. Equally, neglected plants that are weak-growing are themselves prone to disease, completing a vicious cycle. Fortunately, orchid diseases are relatively rare but you may occasionally encounter the symptoms described on these pages. Orchid viruses are usually not treatable and affected plants should be burned to eradicate the disease.

BLACK MOLD

HOW TO IDENTIFY A dark brown or black sooty deposit becomes visible on the upper surfaces of leaves. It generally grows on the sticky honeydew deposits of scale insects or mealybugs (see p.51).
CONTROL In mild cases, the mold can be washed off to reveal a healthy leaf beneath. Severely affected leaves should be cut off and burned.
PREVENTION Find the pests that secreted the honeydew and deal with these as recommended. Also control ants that can spread the pests from plant to plant (see p.51).

Black mold is usually a secondary problem caused by the accumulation of honeydew, in this case produced by aphids, on a leaf surface.

BROWN SPOT

HOW TO IDENTIFY Soft, watery patches appear on leaves, which then turn brown or black and appear sunken. The disease is caused by the bacterium *Pseudomonas cattleyae*. Phalaenopsis and paphiopedilums are particularly vulnerable and can be severely affected.
CONTROL If the affected area is small, treat it with hydrogen peroxide. Otherwise, cut off all affected areas with a clean, sharp knife.
PREVENTION Periodically spray plants that are known to be susceptible with an approved bactericide/fungicide.

Treat plants neighboring an affected orchid because bacteria are spread by water splashes.

CYMBIDIUM MOSAIC VIRUS

HOW TO IDENTIFY Dark, sunken patches appear on the leaves, sometimes in a diamond pattern. Despite the name, all orchids are susceptible.
CONTROL Control is not possible, so all affected plants should be destroyed.
PREVENTION Control insect pests, which sometimes introduce the virus through their mouthparts or allow it to enter plants through the wounds they create. Practice good hygiene when repotting or propagating plants, and sterilize cutting tools while working on plants.

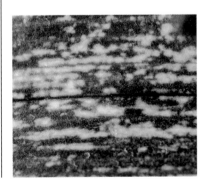

On cymbidium orchids, the first signs of the virus are elongated yellow areas.

BLACK ROT

HOW TO IDENTIFY Soft, dark patches with pale margins appear on leaves. The rot then spreads, affecting rhizomes and roots. The problem is most likely to occur when plants are kept at low temperatures with a humidity level that is too high and with overly wet potting mix.

CONTROL Cut off all affected leaves, sterilizing the blade between cuts. If the rot has reached the rhizome, destroy the entire plant.

PREVENTION Maintain appropriate growing conditions and repot susceptible plants regularly.

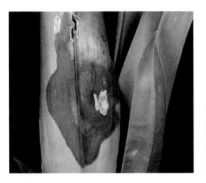

Phalaenopsis and cattleya orchids are especially vulnerable to black rot.

PETAL BLIGHT

HOW TO IDENTIFY Flowers become blotched and marked, with white-flowered cattleyas particularly susceptible. The condition often occurs when plants in flower are exposed to strong sunshine or as a result of other faults in cultivation, such as polluted or stale air or extreme cold and wet.

CONTROL Cut off affected flowers that may otherwise weaken and become vulnerable to disease.

PREVENTION Maintain appropriate growing conditions for plants at all times and ensure that flowers are not in contact with water. Remove faded flowers promptly.

Blight rarely leads to the death of a plant, but it degrades the appearance of the flowers.

LEAF WILT

HOW TO IDENTIFY Leaves droop and may turn yellow; in severe cases they may be shed from the plant. The problem is usually caused by dehydration, especially when coupled with excessively high temperatures; however, overwatering can also produce the same symptoms.

CONTROL Water the plant well by submerging the roots in water for up to 20 minutes. Drain thoroughly and keep the plant cool until the leaves turn green again.

PREVENTION Maintain appropriate growing conditions, especially in summer when the problem is most likely to occur.

Make sure that the plant roots are not standing in water: waterlogging can cause leaf wilt, too.

ABORTED FLOWERS

Flower buds that fail to open can be a problem with certain orchids, particularly phalaenopsis. This is almost invariably down to inappropriate growing conditions, particularly in fall and winter, when light levels and temperatures start to drop. For plants in bud at this time, keep light levels high and avoid overwatering. If you want to move a plant from one location to another to enjoy the flowers, wait until all of them are open.

Buds at the tip of a spike are sometimes shed.

Rarer orchids, such as the Central American species *Prosthechea prismatocarpa*, may only come on the market from time to time when a grower successfully propagates plants.

DIRECTORY OF ORCHIDS

On the following pages, a selection of orchids—focused on those that are generally available in the trade—is described alphabetically by genus. Larger genera have longer introductions that outline the overall characteristics of the genus. For reasons of practicality, certain intergeneric hybrids appear within the entry for the dominant parent genus. For instance, *Aliceara* 'Tahoma Glacier' is included under *Oncidium* because it carries a great deal of genetic material from the oncidiums and has the same cultivation needs, so can be considered alongside them.

ANGRAECUM

These orchids hold a special place in collections, not only for their pristine, scented flowers but also for their scientific associations. *A. sesquipedale* proved significant in the history of evolutionary studies. Charles Darwin (1809–1882) surmised that the long spur on its flower suggested it could only be pollinated by a moth—at the time undiscovered—with an extremely long proboscis. Sure enough, a hawk moth with an appropriately long proboscis was identified 21 years later—vital evidence of how species evolve, and an example of mutual dependence between an orchid and a pollinator.

Angraecum didieri is a species with thick, fleshy flowers from Madagascar.

Angraecum eburneum produces horizontal inflorescences (flower heads) of long-lived, waxy, white flowers.

ABOUT THESE PLANTS

The genus *Angraecum* contains around 200 mainly evergreen, monopodial, usually epiphytic, orchids, most of which are confined to Africa, where they grow in rainforest areas between sea level and 6,600 ft (2,000 m). A few are lithophytes (see p.10). Angraecums lack pseudobulbs; their flower stems instead arise from the base of the leaves, which are semirigid, usually fleshy, and narrowly oblong. Spurred, often starlike, flowers emerge either singly or in clusters, their colors restricted to white, green, and yellowish green. They range from tiny to 8 in (20 cm) across. Many species are under threat of extinction in the wild owing to loss of habitat and over-collection and are the subject of preservation orders. The few species in cultivation need regular care, so are best suited to more experienced growers.

HOW TO GROW

These warm growing orchids need a minimum winter temperature of 64°F (18°C) and a summer maximum of 86°F (30°C). Consistently moist conditions are essential because the plants have no water-storing pseudobulbs. Water the plants freely throughout the year, but reduce watering slightly in winter when the plants are resting (but not if they are still actively growing and flowering). Let containers drain fully after watering to avoid the risk of rotting. In summer, apply a fertilizer at every third watering and mist the plants once or twice daily. Grow in shade year round.

REPOTTING AND PROPAGATION

Plants should be repotted every two to three years when they get top-heavy and the roots fill the container. Note that the presence of aerial roots does not itself indicate that repotting is necessary. With no pseudobulbs, they are unsuitable for division, but some species may produce keikis (see p.44) around the base of the plant, and these may be detached and rooted in standard orchid potting mix.

A. DISTICHUM

HEIGHT 6 in (15 cm)
SPREAD 6 in (15 cm)
FLOWERING Summer–fall
TEMPERATURE Above 64°F (18°C)

This diminutive but surprisingly tough orchid originates in tropical Africa, from Guinea to Uganda and Angola, where it grows in damp, evergreen forests at elevations of 1,950–4,900 ft (600–1,500 m). Leaves, 3¼–4¾ in (8–12 cm) long, are broad and oblong. Night-scented, white flowers ½ in (1 cm) across, are produced singly among the leaves. Mature plants produce flowers in great quantity. Grow in small pots filled with standard orchid potting mix or mounted on a slab of bark.

Flowers of this species are large relative to the size of the plant.

A. SESQUIPEDALE

HEIGHT 24 in (60 cm)
SPREAD 12 in (30 cm)
FLOWERING Winter
TEMPERATURE Above 64°F (18°C)

This robust species from Madagascar is found in forest edges below 400–500 ft (120–150 m). It grows attached to trees by means of fleshy, succulent roots and forms an upright fan of strappy, thick-textured, oblong, dark green leaves up to 12 in (30 cm) long. Flowers 6¾–8¾ in (17–22 cm) across, are produced in clusters of one to four on stems 10–12 in (25–30 cm) long. Waxy and ivory white, they are scented at night. Grow in medium to large pots filled with standard orchid potting mix.

The scented star-like flowers are evenly distributed over the plant.

The bowl-like shape of the yellow flowers has given the plants the name "tulip" or "cradle" orchid.

ANGULOA CLOWESII

HEIGHT 24 in (60 cm)
SPREAD 24 in (60 cm)

FLOWERING Spring–summer
TEMPERATURE Above 52°F (11°C)

The South American genus *Anguloa* comprises some ten species that grow at high altitudes on the forest floor in the Andes, only occasionally epiphytically. Unusually among orchids, they are deciduous, the leaves dying back in the fall. They grow in cool to intermediate conditions.

The most commonly seen species is *A. clowesii*, native to Venezuela and Colombia. This plant forms a cluster of large, conical pseudobulbs and has broad, folded, deep green leaves 18–32 in (45–80 cm) long. Solitary, bright lemon yellow flowers, up to 4 in (10 cm) long, are carried on stems up to 9 in (23 cm) in length. The flowers have a distinctive anise-like scent.

HOW TO GROW *Anguloa clowesii* is cool growing. It should not be exposed to winter temperatures below 52°F (11°C) and must be kept well shaded in summer in temperatures that should not exceed 68°F (20°C). Water plants weekly in spring and summer and add fertilizer at every third watering. In winter, the plants will drop their leaves: allow them to rest, watering only if the pseudobulbs show signs of shriveling. Resume watering when new growth begins. Grow these plants in medium to large pots filled with terrestrial orchid potting mix or a combination of fine bark, perlite, and sphagnum moss. Repot and divide after flowering if necessary.

BLETILLA

Bletillas are attractive plants with elegant bell-shaped flowers and long leaves that remain fresh-looking throughout the growing season. Unlike most commonly sold orchids, they are surprisingly hardy and can—with care—be grown permanently outdoors in a bed or border as long as they are sited in a very sheltered spot. They will grow readily indoors, but the best compromise may be to plant them in containers on a patio or balcony and bring them into an unheated greenhouse or sheltered porch in winter for protection against the wind and cold.

ABOUT THESE PLANTS

Bletilla is a small genus of deciduous sympodial orchids that grow terrestrially in cool, temperate regions of China, Japan, Thailand, Vietnam, and Burma. These vigorous plants have short rhizomes that develop tuberous pseudobulbs, which may be partially below ground. Each clawlike, hard-textured pseudobulb produces three or four leaves. Bell-like flowers develop in loose clusters of up to 12 on upright stems; flowering occurs before the leaves have fully developed.

HOW TO GROW

Bletillas are cool growing, some tolerating winter temperatures as low as 23°F (–10°C). Grow plants in pots, inside or outside, in any good potting mix, ideally with some added leaf mold, and place them in indirect sunlight. Water freely in spring and summer and add fertilizer at every third watering. Keep plants dry in winter when out of leaf. Bring pots under cover before the first frosts.

If planted in the garden, bletillas need moist, well-drained soil and a sheltered position that is part-shaded in summer. In cold areas, you can lift the plants after their leaves have died back and store them in a dry, frost-free, and well-lit place over winter.

The appealing flowers are delicately colored and hang like butterflies in the air.

REPOTTING AND PROPAGATION

Plants that fill their pots can be repotted in spring as they are coming into growth. This may need doing every year. Shake the old potting mix off the roots and cut off and discard any old pseudobulbs that show no signs of new life. Plants can be divided at the same time, using a knife to cut through the rhizome. Pot the divided plants into a standard houseplant potting mix mixed with perlite and fine bark. Plants in the ground can be allowed to develop more sizable clumps and divided every three years.

BLETILLA OCHRACEA

HEIGHT 24 in (60 cm)
SPREAD 12 in (30 cm)
FLOWERING Spring–early summer
TEMPERATURE Above 23°F (–10°C)

Sometimes known as the Chinese butterfly orchid, this species is native to Vietnam and China. Each roughly oval pseudobulb produces three or four folded leaves. Flowers, 1 in (2.5 cm) across, are creamy pale yellow and produced in clusters of 3 to 14 on stems up to 18 in (45 cm) long. The lips are white, conspicuously ruffled, and generously marked with bright yellow-red. Grow in medium pots filled with houseplant potting mix (with additions as recommended opposite).

The flowers of this species are beautifully marked and excellent for cutting.

BLETILLA STRIATA

HEIGHT 12–24 in (30–60 cm)
SPREAD 12–24 in (30–60 cm)
FLOWERING Spring–early summer
TEMPERATURE Above 23°F (–10°C)

This species originates from China and Japan, where it grows in clumps in shady woodland. It has flattened pseudobulbs and ribbed, strappy leaves, 12–18 in (30–45 cm) long. Magenta flowers, 1 in (2.5 cm) across, are carried in clusters of three to seven (sometimes more), opening from the base of the cluster. The lips are furrowed and have darker markings. Grow in medium pots filled with houseplant potting mix (with additions as recommended opposite).

Sometimes known as the "hyacinth orchid," this species is in flower for up to six weeks.

ASPASIA LUNATA

HEIGHT 12 in (30 cm)
SPREAD 8 in (20 cm)
FLOWERING Fall
TEMPERATURE 54°F (12°C)

Aspasia is a small genus, and *A. lunata* is its most widely grown member. This epiphytic, sympodial species is native to tropical forests in Brazil and Bolivia. It has oval, flattened pseudobulbs, each with two short leaves, produced on a creeping rhizome. Spiderlike, green flowers are generously spotted with maroon and have white lips marked with violet. Grow in shade in small pots filled with standard orchid potting mix. Water well in spring and summer, less in winter.

This compact, dense-growing plant makes an excellent choice for a windowsill.

BRASSAVOLA NODOSA

HEIGHT 7 in (18 cm)
SPREAD 7 in (18 cm)
FLOWERING Summer
TEMPERATURE 55°F (13°C)

This epiphyte (sometimes also found growing on rocks) has a range from Mexico to Panama and Venezuela. Its woody, creeping rhizome produces stemlike, cylindrical pseudobulbs with stout, upright leaves. Three to five light green or white flowers, 3¼ in (8 cm) across, are held in clusters up to 6 in (15 cm) in length. The lips are white, spotted with maroon. Grow in small pots of standard orchid potting mix or on a bark slab in good light. Water well in spring–summer and keep dry in winter.

Delicately scented flowers dangle from the stems in loose clusters.

BRASSIA

Sometimes known as spider orchids because of their narrow, elongated petals and sepals, these plants have become popular and widely available. They are eye-catching when in full flower, and the individual blooms are often intriguingly marked, but their principal appeal lies in their scent, which can be intoxicating. Their similarity to spiders is no mere coincidence. In the wild, these plants are pollinated by spider-hunter wasps (*Pepsis*), which attempt to sting what they take to be their prey, transferring pollen from flower to flower in the process.

Carried on airy stems, brassia flowers are often subtly colored and exquisitely marked.

Flowering stems often spread out laterally, with flowers all along their length.

ABOUT THESE PLANTS

Native to the Americas, these sympodial, evergreen, epiphytic orchids have strong aerial roots that anchor them to host trees, although they are occasionally also found rooted in the ground. The genus comprises some 66 species, found at a range of altitudes from sea level upward, the greatest diversity occurring in the Peruvian Andes. Some 90 hybrids have been registered. Brassias form horizontal or upright rhizomes from which arise compressed, roughly oval to rounded or sometimes cylindrical, pseudobulbs, each with one to three strappy leaves. Flower stems, each bearing up to 12 fragrant blooms, emerge from the base of mature pseudobulbs, often upright initially but then arching over at the tip. Sometimes, the weight of the open flowers brings them down virtually to the horizontal.

HOW TO GROW

Brassias are intermediate growing, requiring nighttime temperatures no lower than 54°F (10–12°C) in winter, and summer highs of less than 72°F (22°C). Shade the plants in summer or place them in indirect light to prevent leaf scorch. Move them to a bright position in winter. Water freely when the plants are growing strongly (usually in winter) and feed with a nitrogen-high fertilizer at every third watering. Switch to a high-potassium fertilizer in spring to promote flowering. Rest plants after flowering by reducing watering. Mist them in summer, if necessary, to lower the temperature.

REPOTTING AND PROPAGATION

Brassias need repotting every two to three years—more frequently in the case of fast-growing species. Repot after flowering or just as plants are coming into growth. Plants with roots that fill their pot can be divided at the same time using a knife to slice through the rhizomes. Dormant back bulbs can be removed and potted up separately, provided they are firm and healthy.

B. ARANIA VERDE

HEIGHT 18 in (45 cm)
SPREAD 18 in (45 cm)
FLOWERING Spring
TEMPERATURE Above 52°F (11°C)

A hybrid of B. Rex and the species B. gireoudiana, a native of Costa Rica and Panama, this orchid has roughly oval pseudobulbs and narrowly oval leaves up to 12 in (30 cm) long. Flower clusters, produced on arching stems to 24 in (60 cm) long, comprise six to eight fragrant, pale green, long-lasting flowers. Petals are spotted with reddish chocolate brown in the lower section. This vigorous plant is best grown in a large pot filled with standard orchid potting mix.

Dramatic markings on the flowers make this a very desirable orchid.

B. AURANTIACA

HEIGHT 9 in (23 cm)
SPREAD 6–9 in (15–23 cm)
FLOWERING Spring
TEMPERATURE Above 50°F (10°C)

Found in Colombian, Ecuadorian, and Venezuelan forests at altitudes of 6,600–8,250 ft (2,000–2,500 m), this species produces oblong pseudobulbs, each with two narrowly oval, mid-green leaves, 4 in (10 cm) long. Flower stems arising from the base are upright at first but arch with age, reaching 20 in (50 cm) in length. They hold clusters of orange flowers 1 in (2.5 cm) long. This plant needs space for its spreading leaves. Grow in small pots filled with standard orchid potting mix.

The dense starlike blooms of this orchid form a tasseled orange mass.

B. ORANGE DELIGHT

HEIGHT 12 in (30 cm)
SPREAD 20 in (50 cm)
FLOWERING Summer (usually)
TEMPERATURE Above 52°F (11°C)

The progeny of the species B. aurantiaca and hybrid group B. Mary Traub Levin, this plant has a spreading rhizome and large, oval pseudobulbs. From the tip of each pseudobulb emerges a pair of broad, arching leaves, to 12 in (30 cm) long. A single stem, to 12 in (30 cm) tall, appears at the base of each mature bulb, bearing spidery flowers, 2 in (5 cm) long, that are dark yellow with brown markings that fade to orange. Grow in medium pots filled with standard orchid potting mix.

Strikingly colored flowers have ensured this orchid's popularity.

B. REX

HEIGHT 14 in (35 cm)
SPREAD 20 in (50 cm)
FLOWERING Spring–early summer
TEMPERATURE Above 52°F (11°C)

A primary hybrid of two species, B. verrucosa, and B. gireoudiana, this popular orchid has been widely used in further hybrid production. Pseudobulbs are roughly oval, with strappy, arching, bright green leaves. Flower spikes, to 14 in (35 cm) long, carry up to 20 fragrant, spidery flowers. The pale green sepals are very narrow and are prominently marked with brown bands. Grow this robust plant in a small to medium pot filled with standard orchid potting mix.

B. Rex is deservedly one of the most widely grown brassias.

BULBOPHYLLUM

This genus is the largest in the orchid family and includes some of the most outlandish of all flowers. However, only a small number are commonly cultivated. Bulbophyllums have not been hybridized, so only species are available for purchase. While the flowers of some are sweetly fragrant, others are distinctly offensive; in their native habitat they often are pollinated by flies. Certain species are endangered in the wild and are threatened by habitat loss. There is no "typical" bulbophyllum; the plants included here are among the most suitable for amateur growers.

The sepals of a bulbophyllum flower are often curved and intriguingly marked.

Pseudobulbs are rounded and sometimes clustered on creeping, woody rhizomes.

ABOUT THESE PLANTS

The genus *Bulbophyllum* comprises some 1,000 to 1,200 evergreen, mainly epiphytic, sympodial species that are scattered throughout the tropics and subtropics. They vary in size from plants with pealike pseudobulbs and tiny flowers to *B. fletcherianum*, which can be up to 6 ft (2 m) in length and has huge tonguelike leaves. Roots are threadlike or fibrous so plants can cling on to rocks and trees or hang from branches. The plants have rounded pseudobulbs that are produced on creeping rhizomes, each pseudobulb usually having a single leaf from its top. The leaves are often succulent and have a prominent central fold. At varying times of year, flowering spikes emerge from the bases of pseudobulbs. The flowers are produced either singly or in a cluster or rosette. In most species, the sepals are the showiest part.

HOW TO GROW

Bulbophyllums are cool to intermediate growing. Temperatures should not drop below 55°F (13°C) at night, or rise above 77°F (25°C) by day. Grow them in pots or baskets filled with standard epiphytic orchid potting mix or attach types with pendent stems to bark slabs. In spring and summer, water plants generously and mist twice a day. Feed at every third watering; in spring and early summer use a nitrogen-high feed, then switch to a potassium-high feed to encourage flower development. After flowering, cut flower stems back to the base. Shade in summer and move plants to a lighter position in winter.

REPOTTING AND PROPAGATION

These orchids perform best when pot bound, so repot only when essential. Dividing plants is best done just after flowering; cut through the tough rhizome with a sharp knife or pruners. New plants can also be produced from dormant back bulbs. Remove and pot up back bulbs individually in moss, then grow them on in orchid potting mix as new growth appears.

B. AMBROSIA

HEIGHT 4 in (10 cm)
SPREAD 6 in (15 cm)
FLOWERING Late winter–early spring
TEMPERATURE Above 55°F (13°C)

This orchid originates from China and Vietnam where it grows in evergreen and semi-deciduous forest on limestone cliffs, mossy rocks, and tree bases at elevations of 1,000–4,265 ft (300–1,300m). The diminutive plants have roughly oval, orange-yellow pseudobulbs that are widely spaced on a rhizome. The fragrant, subtly colored flowers, 1¼ in (3 cm) long, are white to pale green and produced singly. Grow in a small hanging pot filled with standard orchid potting mix or attached to a bark slab.

Flowers of this species are exquisitely striped in a red-maroon color.

B. CAREYANUM

HEIGHT 10 in (25 cm)
SPREAD 12 in (30 cm)
FLOWERING Summer
TEMPERATURE Above 55°F (13°C)

This species grows in evergreen lowland forests in the eastern Himalaya, Burma, and Thailand. It produces spherical to oblong, lightly grooved pseudobulbs, each bearing a single, narrow leaf up to 10 in (25 cm) long. Small, fragrant, orange-yellow or green flowers, tinged with red-brown or purple, are densely packed in downward-arching, cone-like clusters to 8 in (20 cm) long. Individual flowers do not open fully. Grow in a small pot filled with standard orchid potting mix.

The shape of the flower clusters has given this plant the name "fir cone orchid."

B. LOBBII

HEIGHT 6 in (15 cm)
SPREAD 9 in (23 cm)
FLOWERING Early summer
TEMPERATURE Above 55°F (13°C)

This orchid is native to parts of India and southeast Asia down to the Philippines, growing in forests at altitudes of around 650–6,500 ft (200–2,000m). It has roughly oval pseudobulbs, each with a narrowly oval leaf, 4 in (10 cm) long. Solitary flowers, 2¾–4 in (7–10 cm) across, are fragrant and ocher-yellow, speckled with red, and are carried on stems 6 in (15 cm) long. Grow these plants in small pots filled with standard orchid potting mix and, for the best results, ensure consistently warm conditions.

Striking flowers have made this species the most widely grown bulbophyllum.

B. MACRANTHUM

HEIGHT 8 in (20 cm)
SPREAD 5 in (12 cm)
FLOWERING Spring and fall
TEMPERATURE Above 55°F (13°C)

Found from sea level to altitudes of 5,000 ft (1,500m) in Assam, Borneo, and Cambodia, this small orchid produces a stout, hairy rhizome with well spaced, roughly oval pseudobulbs. Each one carries a single, oblong, fleshy leaf that is up to 6 in (15 cm) long. Fleshy flowers, to 2¼ in (6 cm) across, are held among the leaves. Heavily speckled with dark red, they have glowing yellow centers. Grow this plant on a slab of bark or in a shallow basket filled with standard orchid potting mix.

Rather oddly, the flowers of this species are held upside down.

CALANTHE

Plants in the genus *Calanthe* originate from both tropical and temperate areas, but only a handful of species (and their hybrids) are grown by orchid enthusiasts, with evergreens particularly popular in Japan. Calanthes are fast-growing, have a relatively short season, and need adequate headroom to accommodate their tall stems. Some cool-growing calanthes are suitable for planting outdoors in mild, sheltered areas, in well-drained soil, and in partial or dappled shade. They are often easier to grow in pots in a cold conservatory or greenhouse.

Calanthe flowers are generously produced and can last for several weeks.

Grouped together outdoors, calanthes can put on an impressive display.

ABOUT THESE PLANTS

Calanthes are mostly terrestrial plants that come from a variety of climatic zones in Asia, Polynesia, and Madagascar. Some grow at sea level, others in lowland forests to altitudes of 10,000 ft (3,000 m), where conditions are generally cooler. They can be evergreen, semievergreen, or deciduous. The deciduous types typically originate in woodlands or grow among shaded rocks.

The pseudobulbs of calanthes are crowded, angular, and sometimes partially buried, with thick roots. They produce clusters of two to five folded leaves that taper toward the base.

Flowers are spread along tall, arching spikes that emerge from the bases of pseudobulbs during fall and winter. The sepals and petals are relatively narrow and widely spread, while lips, which are often elongated, have three or four spreading lobes. In most species, there is a spur at the base of the flower.

HOW TO GROW

Depending on the species, calanthes can be cool growing, tolerating temperatures as low as 14°F (−10°C), or warm growing, needing a winter minimum of 64°F (18°C), with a summer maximum of 86°F (30°C). Grow them in terrestrial orchid potting mix in terra-cotta pots, which provide ballast for the tall, rapidly growing stems. Place plants in bright, filtered light in a humid environment. Water them freely in summer and apply fertilizer at every second or third watering, using a high-nitrogen type in spring and early summer, then switching to a high-potassium type in late summer and fall to encourage flowering. In winter, water evergreens sparingly, but keep deciduous types dry while they are out of leaf.

REPOTTING AND PROPAGATION

Pot plants on annually, using fresh potting mix, in early spring when the new growth starts to emerge. Congested plants can be divided at the same time, using a sharp knife to separate the pseudobulbs.

C. DISCOLOR

HEIGHT 6–12 in (15–30 cm)
SPREAD 12 in (30 cm)
FLOWERING Spring
TEMPERATURE Above 23°F (–10°C)

This evergreen or semi-evergreen species is native to Korea and Japan, where it grows close to streams in damp, shady, low altitude rainforest. *C. discolor* has narrow, strappy leaves around 8–12 in (20–30 cm) in length and upright stems, to 16 in (40 cm) tall. These carry clusters of up to ten purple-brown to green flowers, 1–1½ in (2.5–4 cm) across, which have pale rose pink or white lips. Grow in small to medium pots filled with terrestrial orchid potting mix.

If planted outdoors, this orchid will naturalize and spread by means of offsets.

C. STRIATA

HEIGHT 24–32 in (60–80 cm)
SPREAD 16–20 in (40–50 cm)
FLOWERING Late spring–early summer
TEMPERATURE Above 23°F (–10°C)

This deciduous terrestrial orchid is found in Korea and Japan. It has small, roughly oval pseudobulbs, each of which has two or three strongly ribbed leaves that can reach 10–20 in (25–50 cm) in length. Its upright stems, to 32 in (80 cm) long, carry up to 20 fragrant flowers 1½–2¾ in (4–7 cm) across. The flowers open before new leaves appear; sepals and petals are yellow to brownish-yellow, while the lips are clear yellow. Grow in a large pot filled with terrestrial orchid potting mix.

The brightly colored flowers have a delicate citrusy fragrance.

CALYPSO BULBOSA

HEIGHT 8 in (20 cm)
SPREAD 6 in (15 cm)
FLOWERING Summer
TEMPERATURE Above –4°F (–20°C)

The orchid genus *Calypso* contains just this one species, which occurs in damp woodland, bogs, and marshes in Europe, Asia, and North America. An underground corm produces a single, pleated leaf, to 4¾ in (12 cm) long, followed by a nodding, slipper-like fragrant flower. The bloom is reddish-purple or white, with white lips and is carried on a slender stem, 4–8 in (10–20 cm) high. Grow in filtered light in small pots filled with terrestrial orchid potting mix, watering freely when in growth.

This orchid can be grown successfully outdoors in a sheltered spot in moist soil.

CATTLEYA

Among the most flamboyant of all orchids, cattleyas were historically prized by plant hunters and growers, and have been adopted as the national flowers of several South American counties. Their sumptuous blooms and tendency to grow in large colonies have led to over-collection from their natural habitats, and the status of many is endangered. The group includes not only members of the genus *Cattleya*, but also hybrids made with other genera that produce even more showy flowers.

ABOUT THESE PLANTS

Cattleya is a South American genus of evergreen epiphytes naturally found from sea level to altitudes of 7,000 ft (2,000 m), where they often grow along mountain streams. Most have erect, stout to slender, oval pseudobulbs produced on short, horizontal rhizomes (*see p.14*). From each pseudobulb emerge one or two leaves that are leathery in texture and usually mid- to dark-green. Flowers are produced in clusters of two to four. The lip of the flower often has a different coloration from the rest of the bloom, producing striking visual contrast.

Included in the following section are some examples of *Guarianthe*, plants that were formerly part of *Cattleya* but now occupy a genus of their own. Many hundreds of hybrids are available. Crosses with *Guarianthe* have produced × *Cattlianthe*, while × *Rhyncholaeliocattleya* has resulted from crossing with *Rhyncholaelia*. For convenience, the name "cattleya" is applied to all these orchids.

HOW TO GROW

Cattleyas can be grown in standard orchid containers or baskets filled with epiphytic orchid potting mix. Keep them in bright light in spring–summer, but screened from scorching sunlight. Allow them full light in winter. They appreciate high humidity, but the air must not be allowed to become stagnant, so good ventilation is necessary. Water plants weekly in spring and summer, when they should be growing strongly: reduce frequency to every two to three weeks at other times. For best results, feed plants with a high-nitrogen fertilizer every two to three waterings in spring–summer, switching to a high-potash fertilizer in late summer to fall. Remove flowers and stalks as they fade, trimming back to the tops of the pseudobulbs. Plants benefit from complete rest in winter after which they should grow and flower in the next year with renewed vigor. You can induce dormancy by withholding water for a six-week period (*see p.35*).

REPOTTING AND PROPAGATION

Mature plants can develop many pseudobulbs. If there are more than eight, and the roots are flowing over the sides of the pot, plants should be divided. They are typically ready for this every two to three years. Plants should not be divided when flowering—the optimum time for this is immediately after flowering but before new buds develop. A sharp knife may be needed to cut through the stout rhizomes. The plants can also be propagated from dormant back bulbs, provided these are firm and healthy.

THE CORSAGE ORCHID

Cattleyas are a favorite choice for use in corsages and are associated with love and pleasure. They feature, for example, in Marcel Proust's epic novel *À la recherche du temps perdu*, where Odette de Crécy, the love interest of protagonist Charles Swann, wears the flowers in a corsage attached to her bodice. After her corsage becomes dislodged in a moment of passion, "doing a cattleya" becomes their code for lovemaking.

A corsage featuring cattleyas is decorative and highly scented.

Cattleya flowers are typically large and often have frilled edges.

C. BICOLOR

HEIGHT 4 ft (1.2 m)
SPREAD 18 in (45 cm)
FLOWERING Summer–fall
TEMPERATURE Above 41°F (5°C)

This robust species is found in a range of habitats in its native Brazil. Its clustered, cylindrical, grooved pseudobulbs each produce two oblong leaves, 4¾–8 in (12–20 cm) long. Heavy-textured, very fragrant, yellow-green flowers, 4 in (10 cm) across, have bright crimson lips and are produced in clusters of three to five on short spikes. The plant is very popular, not least because it is relatively easy to grow and its bright blooms are long lasting. Grow it in a large container filled with standard orchid potting mix.

This distinctive orchid produces firm-textured flowers.

C. CHIC BONNET

HEIGHT 14 in (35 cm)
SPREAD 12 in (30 cm)
FLOWERING Spring–summer
TEMPERATURE Above 52°F (11°C)

Produced by crossing C. Easter Bonnet with C. Chickamauga, this hybrid produces clusters of luminous rich pink flowers. The blooms are carried among stiffly upright, oblong leaves and are around 5 in (12 cm) across, with ruffled edges. Their lips are hot cerise pink, marked centrally with yellow and edged with pink, and also ruffled at the margin. Chic Bonnet has itself been used to produce further hybrids. Grow it in a medium pot filled with standard orchid potting mix.

This glamorous orchid makes an excellent florist's flower.

C. LABIATA

HEIGHT 12 in (30 cm)
SPREAD 12 in (30 cm)
FLOWERING Fall
TEMPERATURE 41°F (5°C)

This species grows naturally in trees and on rocks in northeastern Brazil. It has club-shaped pseudobulbs, each producing a single oblong leaf up to 12 in (30 cm) in length. Its scented, ruffled, pale rose-pink to lilac-magenta flowers, 6 in (16 cm) across, have purple, yellow-veined lips and are produced in clusters of up to four or five. *C. labiata* is the only large-flowered cattleya species that flowers in the fall. Grow it in small to medium pots filled with standard orchid potting mix.

The long-lasting flowers have an elusive, slightly spicy fragrance that is strongest in the morning.

C. LEOPOLDII

HEIGHT 16 in (40 cm)
SPREAD 6–8 in (15–20 cm)
FLOWERING Late spring–early summer
TEMPERATURE Above 55°F (13°C)

This southern Brazilian species grows naturally in coastal forests at altitudes below 300 ft (100 m). Each of its narrowly cylindrical pseudobulbs produces two oblong leaves, above which appear clusters of three to ten thick-textured, fragrant flowers. Around 4 in (10 cm) across, they are green, heavily and irregularly spotted with dark maroon, and have bright fuchsia pink lips, the color fading to light rose-lilac toward the base. Grow in small to medium pots filled with standard orchid potting mix.

The lightly fragrant spotted flowers are produced in midsummer.

C. LUTEOLA

HEIGHT 6 in (15 cm)
SPREAD 6 in (15 cm)
FLOWERING Late summer–fall
TEMPERATURE Above 41°F (5°C)

This diminutive species found in the lowland Amazonian rainforests of Brazil, Peru, Ecuador, and Bolivia has ridged, cylindrical pseudobulbs, each producing a single, oblong leaf. Waxy, fragrant flowers, to 3¼ in (8 cm) across, are yellow to yellow-green. The lips are often spotted or streaked with crimson and ruffled at the edges. Grow in small pots filled with standard orchid potting mix or on a bark slab.

This compact plant is the parent of many other miniature cattleya hybrids.

C. MAXIMA

HEIGHT 24 in (60 cm)
SPREAD 12 in (30 cm)
FLOWERING Fall–winter
TEMPERATURE Above 41°F (5°C)

This species is from Ecuador, Colombia, and Peru, where it grows epiphytically at elevations of 300–6,000 ft (100–1,800 m). Each club-shaped pseudobulb produces a single, broadly oblong leaf. Flower spikes up to 8 in (20 cm) long carry three to six fragrant, wavy-edged flowers, to 6 in (15 cm) across. Funnel-like lips, to 2½ in (7 cm) long, are pale pink and veined with purple, with a central yellow streak. Grow in small to medium pots filled with standard orchid potting mix.

The pale pink to lilac flowers last long on the plant but have little scent.

C. TRIANAE

HEIGHT 12 in (30 cm)
SPREAD 12 in (30 cm)
FLOWERING Winter–spring
TEMPERATURE Above 41°F (5°C)

This species is from Colombia, where it grows in cloud forests at altitudes of 5,000–6,500 ft (1,500–2,000 m). It has club-shaped pseudobulbs, from each of which emerges a single, succulent, oblong leaf, 12 in (30 cm) long. The flowers are 8 in (20 cm) across and have well-spaced petals and sepals. White or rose-white, often with a purple flush, they have pink and magenta ruffle-edged lips. Plants are slow growing. Grow in small to medium pots filled with standard orchid potting mix.

The elegant bloom of this species is the national flower of its native Colombia.

C. WARSCEWICZII

HEIGHT 24 in (60 cm)
SPREAD 18 in (45 cm)
FLOWERING Summer
TEMPERATURE Above 52°F (11°C)

In its native Colombia, this orchid grows epiphytically at elevations of 1,650–5,500 ft (500–1,700 m). Its slender, cylindrical pseudobulbs each carry a single leaf, while upright flower spikes, which may be 18 in (45 cm) tall, have up to ten fragrant, rose pink blooms. The blooms are 12 in (30 cm) across with lips 3 in (8 cm) long; they are carmine pink, blotched with yellow in the throat and have ruffled edges. Grow in medium to large pots filled with standard orchid potting mix.

This species has the largest flowers of any cattleya and has been much used in breeding.

Cattleya trianae is best grown in bright, indirect light.

CATTLIANTHE HAZEL BOYD 'APRICOT GLOW'

HEIGHT 12 in (30 cm)
SPREAD 8 in (20 cm)
FLOWERING Spring–early summer
TEMPERATURE Above 41°F (5°C)

Crossing *Cattleya* with *Guarianthe* produced the hybrid genus *Cattlianthe*. 'Apricot Glow' is a member of a group made from a further cross between *Cattleya* California Apricot and *Cattlianthe* Jewel Box. Its apricot-orange flowers are around 3½ in (9 cm) across and marked with crimson on their lips. Grow in small to medium pots filled with standard orchid potting mix. For best results, allow the potting mix to dry out between waterings.

The vivid flowers are produced in small clusters on a compact plant.

GUARIANTHE AURANTIACA

HEIGHT 12 in (30 cm)
SPREAD 12 in (30 cm)
FLOWERING Summer
TEMPERATURE Above 41°F (5°C)

This species, which was formerly considered a member of the genus *Cattleya*, is native to Central America, where it grows epiphytically in rain forests. Its cylindrical or spindle-shaped pseudobulbs produce two roughly oval leaves, each 4–8 in (10–20 cm) long. Flowers, which are around 1½ in (4 cm) across, can be bright orange, red, or pale yellow-gold, often with dark red spots or streaks on the lips, and are carried in generous clusters. Grow in medium pots filled with standard orchid potting mix.

Flowers of this desirable species are relatively small but are produced in abundance.

GUARIANTHE BOWRINGIANA

HEIGHT 3 ft (1 m)
SPREAD 18 in (45 cm)
FLOWERING Fall–winter
TEMPERATURE Above 41°F (5°C)

This species, formerly classified within *Cattleya*, is found in Guatemala and Belize, where it grows both epiphytically and terrestrially on rocky cliffs at elevations of 690–3,000 ft (210–900 m). It has cylindrical pseudobulbs, each producing two narrowly oblong, dark green leaves, 4¾–8 in (12–20 cm) long. Long flower stems carry clusters of gleaming, rose-pink to magenta flowers, 3¼ in (8 cm) across. They have dark purple lips with white throats. Grow in medium to large containers filled with standard orchid potting mix.

Flower spikes can each carry up to 15 luminous pink blooms.

RHYNCHOLAELIOCATTLEYA ST. HELIER

HEIGHT 18 in (45 cm)
SPREAD 18 in (45 cm)
FLOWERING Spring
TEMPERATURE Above 55°F (13°C)

The hybrid genus *Rhyncholaeliocattleya* is a result of a marriage between *Cattleya* and *Rhyncholaelia,* and the group St. Helier is a cross between Norman's Bay and Sussex. One or two narrowly oblong leaves emerge from each of the plant's stout, club-shaped pseudobulbs. Flowers are 6–7 in (15–18 cm) across, and rich pinkish magenta in color with mauve-purple and golden yellow lips. Grow in medium to large pots filled with standard orchid potting mix.

Ruffled edges add to the appeal of these impressive flowers.

COELOGYNE

Coelogynes in full bloom never fail to impress—and not just because these orchids flower when so many others are dormant. Their sweetly fragrant flowers attract admiration as well as a range of pollinating insects, such as bees, wasps, and beetles. The plants are sometimes called "rag orchids" in reference to the frilled edges of their flowers, while those species with pendent flower clusters are commonly named "necklace orchids." Coelogynes are deservedly popular, although they have not yet been subjected to the same heavy hybridizing as other orchid genera.

Coelogyne nitida is a Himalayan species often seen in collections.

Pseudobulbs are often egg-shaped and can vary in size relative to the plant.

ABOUT THESE PLANTS

This genus contains more than 100 species of evergreen, sympodial, spreading epiphytes. They grow at a range of altitudes from lowland forests upward, in regions of India and southeast Asia to the Pacific islands. Occasionally, some species are found growing terrestrially or even as lithophytes on rocks in open, humid habitats. Size varies, but all have pseudobulbs that produce two strappy, leathery-textured, pleated leaves. The pseudobulbs themselves vary in size and may be closely or widely spaced on the rhizome. Flowers, which can appear at any time of year, are often produced in quantity and can be large and showy and have striking markings. Coelogynes can sometimes flower for several weeks at a time, and may even repeat flower, which makes them very desirable as houseplants.

HOW TO GROW

Coelogynes are cool to intermediate growing tropical species. This means that they require a minimum winter nighttime temperature of 59°F (10–15°C). Water well in summer and maintain humidity by misting once or twice daily: feed at every third watering. Place plants in full light in winter.

Allow these orchids to rest after flowering by reducing watering amounts. Intermediate growing types should be kept moist even in winter but others can be allowed to dry out, unless they are flowering. Keep an eye on the pseudobulbs in winter; if they start to shrivel, water the plant.

REPOTTING AND PROPAGATION

Repot every two to three years, when the plant fills its container; do this just after flowering. Alternatively, to produce display plants, repot less frequently and allow the orchid to form large clumps. To propagate, you can divide the plants in mid-spring or, alternatively, remove dormant back bulbs (provided they are firm and healthy) and pot them up separately.

C. CRISTATA

HEIGHT 12 in (30 cm)
SPREAD 24 in (60 cm)
FLOWERING Winter–spring
TEMPERATURE Above 50°F (10°C)

Probably the most popular of the coelogynes, this species is native to cool, moist areas in the eastern Himalaya, where it flowers just before the snows begin to melt. The rounded pseudobulbs produce narrow, arching, dark green leaves, to 12 in (30 cm) long. Hanging flower spikes carry strongly fragrant, pure white, ruffle-edged flowers, 3 in (8 cm) across, with yellow markings in the lips. Grow in medium to large pots filled with standard orchid potting mix and keep in a well-ventilated environment.

A well-rested plant will produce plentiful white blooms in winter.

C. FLACCIDA

HEIGHT 10 in (25 cm)
SPREAD 12 in (30 cm)
FLOWERING Winter–early summer
TEMPERATURE Above 50°F (10°C)

This orchid is from the Himalaya, where it grows in forests at altitudes of 3,000–6,500 ft (900–2,000 m). It has conical pseudobulbs and somewhat oval, semirigid leaves, to 18 in (45 cm) long. The strongly fragrant white flowers are around 1½ in (4 cm) across. They have yellow markings on the central lobe of each lip and reddish brown marks on the lateral lobes and are produced on upright to arching spikes. Grow in small to medium pots filled with standard orchid potting mix.

Widely available, C. flaccida is a shade-loving plant with a strong but not sweet fragrance.

C. MOOREANA 'WESTONBERT'

HEIGHT 24 in (60 cm)
SPREAD 24 in (60 cm)
FLOWERING Spring–early summer
TEMPERATURE Above 59°F (15°C)

This orchid is a cultivar of a species originally found in wet areas of Vietnam, where it grows in cloud forests at altitudes of 4,000–4,265 ft (1,200–1,300 m). Its pseudobulbs are furrowed and the narrow, glossy green leaves are pointed, reaching 15¾ in (40 cm) in length. Flower spikes are upright, to 20 in (5 cm) long; from each one dangle four to eight fragrant, white flowers, with a dark orange disk in the throat. Grow this orchid in a large pot filled with standard orchid potting mix.

This plant reliably produces large white blooms early in the year, making it very popular.

C. SPECIOSA

HEIGHT 12 in (30 cm)
SPREAD 24 in (60 cm)
FLOWERING Any time of year
TEMPERATURE Above 59°F (15°C)

This species originates from the rainforests of Sumatra and Java, where it grows at altitudes of 2,300–6,500 ft (700–2,000 m). It has conical, clustering pseudobulbs and leaves up to 14 in (35 cm) in length. Its musky-scented flowers look somewhat like flying insects. Around 2¾ in (7 cm) across, they vary in color from greenish yellow to pale salmon pink, with reddish brown lips, and are produced in hanging clusters of one to three. Grow in large pots or sturdy baskets filled with orchid potting mix.

The drooping flowers prevent rain from washing away pollen in monsoon conditions.

CYMBIDIUM

Cymbidiums rival phalaenopsis in popularity and are just as easy to grow. They are robust plants that produce upright spikes holding generous numbers of wax-textured flowers. Plants sold in garden centers are often unnamed, as they are easy to produce in quantity for the floristry trade, but it is well worth looking out for rarer named types. A mature cymbidium makes a striking plant for exhibition, either in a cool conservatory or at a plant show. Miniatures make delightful windowsill plants.

A PRIZED PLANT

Well before orchids came to the attention of gardeners in the west, cymbidiums already had a long history in China and are known to have been grown during the Jin dynasty (266–420 CE). Throughout the Far East, they have long been exchanged as symbols of friendship, rare forms with variegated leaves being particularly prized.

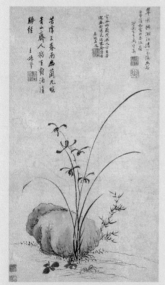

This painting titled *Orchid and Rock* dates back to 16th century China.

ABOUT THESE PLANTS

The genus *Cymbidium* is made up of around 50 species that grow epiphytically, in the ground, or on rocks in both temperate and tropical areas of India, China, Japan, and southeast Asia. From this surprisingly small number of species, breeders have produced a huge range of hybrids, from miniatures to statuesque plants with stems up to 3 ft (1 m) long that bear many flowers.

Cymbidiums have rounded to oval pseudobulbs, and strappy, usually arching, leaves that generally persist for several years on the plant. Flowers are produced in clusters of up to 12 on spikes that appear at the bases of the pseudobulbs toward the end of winter. The blooms, which can last for several months, are held well above the foliage and can be delicately scented. Petals and sepals are often similar in appearance and color but the lips can be contrasting and strikingly marked. Many of the flowers of modern hybrids are thick-textured, making them ideal for floral displays for which plants have to be transported over a long distance.

HOW TO GROW

Cymbidiums are cool growing orchids, needing a winter minimum temperature of 50°F (10°C) with a summer maximum of 60–70°F (16–21°C). Most can be grown in either epiphytic or terrestrial orchid potting mix. Epiphytic potting mix drains more freely but must be pressed firmly around the roots. Many cymbidiums are tall growing, and these varieties should be placed in terra-cotta or other substantial pots that provide good ballast to stop them falling over.

Grow plants in good light, filtering it in summer to prevent scorching. Place in full light in winter. Water freely in spring and summer, adding fertilizer at every third watering. Mist once or twice a day. Water at other times to keep the potting mix barely moist. Flower stems should be supported. Insert canes into the potting mix as flowering stems emerge in mid- to late winter.

REPOTTING AND PROPAGATION

Regular repotting is necessary, otherwise dormant back bulbs may become crowded and the plant will become less productive over time. Repot congested plants in early or mid-spring, immediately after flowering, usually every two to three years. Plants can be divided at the same time, but to develop large, impressive specimens, repot into larger containers without dividing (though dormant back bulbs can be removed). When splitting a plant, use a sharp knife to separate the pseudobulbs. Pot up firm, healthy back bulbs to produce new plants. Older, soft, or withered back bulbs should be discarded.

Orchids such as _Cymbidium_ Burgundian produce heavy blooms on tall stems, so need support.

C. CANALICULATUM

HEIGHT 28 in (70 cm)
SPREAD 28 in (70 cm)
FLOWERING Fall–winter
TEMPERATURE Above 50°F (10°C)

This epiphytic species grows in the forks or hollows of trees in woodland areas of Australia. It forms dense clumps of narrowly oval pseudobulbs from which emerge bladelike leaves, up to 26 in (65 cm) long. The flowers, some 1¾ in (4 cm) across, are produced on arching stems. The blooms are olive green to pale bronze, with a red-brown center. The lips are ivory white, spotted with purple or red. Grow in medium to large pots filled with standard orchid potting mix.

The unusual coloration of the flowers make this orchid a collector's favorite.

C. CASTLE OF MEY 'PINKIE'

HEIGHT 28 in (70 cm)
SPREAD 12 in (30 cm)
FLOWERING Winter–spring
TEMPERATURE Above 50°F (10°C)

This orchid is a selected form of a hybrid group that was bred from C. Putana and C. Western Rose. It is a compact plant with densely packed, rounded pseudobulbs and narrow, arching, strappy leaves that may be up to 20 in (50 cm) long. Slightly arching spikes carry warm rose-pink flowers that measure 2 in (5 cm) across. The paler lips are conspicuously spotted with red and have yellow centers. Grow in medium pots filled with standard orchid potting mix.

This dense-growing cymbidium makes an excellent choice for a house plant.

C. DEVONIANUM

HEIGHT 12 in (30 cm)
SPREAD 12 in (30 cm)
FLOWERING Spring–summer
TEMPERATURE Above 50°F (10°C)

This epiphytic species comes from northeast India and northern Thailand, where it grows on trees and mossy rocks in forests at altitudes of 3,300–6,500 ft (1,000–2,000 m). It has small, roughly oval pseudobulbs and oval leaves, 12–24 in (30–60 cm) long. Its trailing stems carry an abundance of freckled, olive brown to yellow-green flowers, 1½ in (4 cm) across. The lips are a pale to dark spotted purple. Grow in small to medium pots or in a sturdy hanging basket filled with standard orchid potting mix.

Trailing flower stems make this cymbidium ideal for planting in a hanging basket.

C. ERYTHROSTYLUM

HEIGHT 24 in (60 cm)
SPREAD 24 in (60 cm)
FLOWERING Spring–summer
TEMPERATURE Above 50°F (10°C)

Found in Vietnam at elevations of around 5,000 ft (1,500 m), this species grows on trees, on rocks, and also in the ground. The narrowly oval pseudobulbs are flattened, each producing six to eight slender, arching leaves, 18 in (45 cm) long. Its upright to arching spikes, 24 in (60 cm) long, carry four to ten long-lasting, white flowers that may be 2⅓ in (6 cm) across. Lips are pale and patterned with broken pink-red lines. Grow in medium pots filled with standard orchid potting mix.

This attractive species has long-lived blooms: it is the parent of many hybrids.

C. ELEGANS

HEIGHT 20 in (50 cm)
SPREAD 24 in (60 cm)
FLOWERING Fall–winter
TEMPERATURE Above 50°F (10°C)

This epiphytic species is found in the Himalaya and southwest China, where it grows on trees and rocks in shady and damp locations at elevations of 5,000–9,000 ft (1,500–2,800 m). It has slender, roughly oval pseudobulbs and narrowly oval leaves up to 20 in (50 cm) long. Upright spikes carry dense clusters of corn yellow flowers that measure 2 in (5 cm) long; the spikes arch over as the flowers develop. Grow in medium to large pots filled with standard orchid potting mix.

The bell-like flowers of this species, quite unlike other cymbidiums, never open fully.

C. HOOKERIANUM

HEIGHT 24 in (60 cm)
SPREAD 36 in (90 cm)
FLOWERING Early winter
TEMPERATURE Above 50°F (10°C)

This species is found in the Himalaya (it is widespread in Bhutan) and southwest China, and grows epiphytically or lithophytically in cool temperate forests. It has roughly oval pseudobulbs and narrow, arching, strappy leaves that reach lengths of 24 in (60 cm). Arching spikes carry fragrant, deep apple-green flowers that grow to a diameter of 3½–5 in (9–13 cm). Their white lips have ruffled edges and are spotted with purple and yellow. Grow in large pots filled with standard orchid potting mix.

The nodding, highly scented flowers have distinctive three-lobed lips, spotted with pink and red.

C. INSIGNE 'MRS. CARL HOLMES'

HEIGHT 36 in (90 cm)
SPREAD 24 in (60 cm)
FLOWERING Spring
TEMPERATURE Above 50°F (10°C)

This orchid is a cultivar derived from a species found in Vietnam, Thailand, and southern China, where it grows as a lithophyte or terrestrially in open woodland at altitudes of 2,500–5,500 ft (750–1,700 m). Its pseudobulbs are roughly oval, with narrow, strappy, arching leaves that reach lengths of 20–39 in (50–100 cm). The flowers, 3¼ in (8 cm) across, are rose pink, with red-spotted, white lips. Grow these orchids in large pots filled with standard orchid potting mix.

The sepals of this attractive cymbidium curl elegantly inward.

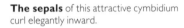

C. KING'S LOCH 'COOKSBRIDGE'

HEIGHT 24 in (60 cm)
SPREAD 36 in (90 cm)
FLOWERING Winter
TEMPERATURE Above 50°F (10°C)

Kings Loch is a hybrid of C. King Arthur and C. Loch Lomond, 'Cooksbridge' being a selection from this hybrid group. The roughly oval pseudobulbs of this orchid produce narrow, arching, strappy leaves, to 24 in (60 cm) in length. Upright spikes carry bright yellow-green flowers, 3¼ in (8 cm) across, which are marked with darker veins. The white lips are patterned in reddish purple toward their edges. Grow in a large pot filled with standard orchid potting mix.

This impressive plant is one of the best known of all the cymbidium hybrids.

C. MIGHTY REMUS

HEIGHT 36 in (90 cm)
SPREAD 36 in (90 cm)
FLOWERING Winter
TEMPERATURE Above 50°F (10°C)

The name of this hybrid reflects its parentage—it is derived from *C.* Remus and *C.* Mighty Mouse. The orchid has roughly oval to rounded pseudobulbs and arching, narrow, strappy leaves that reach lengths of 30 in (75 cm). Its upright spikes are packed with flowers, 3½ in (9 cm) across. Opening yellow-green, they mature to bronze, then orange. The lips are heavily edged and spotted with dark red and have yellow throats. Grow in medium to large pots filled with standard orchid potting mix.

The flowers of this fascinating variety change color as they mature.

C. PONTAC 'MONT MILLAIS'

HEIGHT 36 in (90 cm)
SPREAD 36 in (90 cm)
FLOWERING Winter
TEMPERATURE Above 50°F (10°C)

This orchid is a selection from a group produced by crossing *C.* Memoria Doctor Borg with *C.* Hamsey. Its pseudobulbs are roughly oval, and the narrow, arching leaves that emerge from them can reach lengths of 30 in (75 cm). Tall upright spikes carry clustering, dark red flowers, 4 in (10 cm) across. The lips are white, but generously banded with deep red, a narrow white rim showing at the edges. Grow in large pots filled with standard orchid potting mix.

Richly colored, overlapping flowers give this orchid great presence.

C. PORTELET BAY

HEIGHT 24 in (60 cm)
SPREAD 36 in (90 cm)
FLOWERING Winter
TEMPERATURE Above 50°F (10°C)

Crossing C. Snow Sprite with C. Caithness produced this fine hybrid. The orchid has roughly oval pseudobulbs and strappy, narrow, arching leaves, which can reach a length of 30 in (75 cm). Upright spikes carry well-spaced, white flowers with diameters of 3¼ in (8 cm); these have slightly wavy-edged petals and sepals. The lips, which are ruffled at the margins, are generously striped with red and have prominent yellow centers. Grow these plants in large pots filled with standard orchid potting mix.

The long-lasting blooms of this hybrid are often used in flower arrangements.

C. ROSANETTE

HEIGHT 18 in (45 cm)
SPREAD 18 in (45 cm)
FLOWERING Winter
TEMPERATURE Above 50°F (10°C)

A hybrid of C. Mignonette and C. Vieux Rose, this orchid has roughly oval pseudobulbs and narrow, arching, strappy leaves that grow to 18 in (45 cm) in length. Upright spikes carry soft rose-pink flowers that display delicate darker veins. Lips are white spotted with red, and have yellow centers. They are ruffled toward the edges. A compact habit makes this variety ideal for use as a houseplant. Grow in medium pots filled with standard orchid potting mix.

Rosanette is one of the smaller cymbidiums; it is notably free flowering.

C. SHOWGIRL

HEIGHT 18 in (45 cm)
SPREAD 18 in (45 cm)
FLOWERING Winter–spring
TEMPERATURE Above 50°F (10°C)

This hybrid was produced by crossing C. Sweetheart with C. Alexanderi. It has spherical pseudobulbs and narrow, strappy leaves that reach lengths of up to 18 in (45 cm). It produces upright spikes of ivory white flowers some 2½ in (6 cm) across. Each bloom is strongly flushed with pink, darkening toward the base. The lips are generously flecked and striped with red, making a dramatic contrast. The flowers are excellent for cutting. Grow in medium to large pots filled with standard orchid potting mix.

Firm in texture, the flowers are ideal for a corsage or buttonhole.

C. STRATHBRAAN

HEIGHT 18 in (45 cm)
SPREAD 18 in (45 cm)
FLOWERING Winter
TEMPERATURE Above 50°F (10°C)

A hybrid of *C.* Putana and *C.* New Dimension, this orchid has spherical pseudobulbs and narrow, strappy leaves, to 18 in (45 cm) long. The flower spikes are upright at first but arch as they develop, weighed down by the abundant blooms. These are around 2½ in (6 cm) in diameter and colored pale pink to rose-pink; their irregularly red-flecked lips contrast strongly with the sepals and petals. This orchid is ideal for use in floral design. Grow it in a medium pot filled with standard orchid potting mix.

When fully open, the flowers can weigh down the tips of the flowering spike.

C. STRATHDON 'COOKSBRIDGE NOEL'

HEIGHT 18 in (45 cm)
SPREAD 18 in (45 cm)
FLOWERING Winter
TEMPERATURE Above 50°F (10°C)

This orchid is derived from the Strathdon group, which was produced by crossing *C.* Nip and *C.* Kurun. It has spherical pseudobulbs and strappy, narrow, arching leaves up to 18 in (45 cm) in length. It produces sturdy, upright spikes of showy, firm-textured, dusky red-pink flowers, 2½ in (6 cm) across. The lips are yellow, marked with deep red and pale pink. It is a robust hybrid that makes an excellent house plant. Grow in medium pots filled with standard orchid potting mix.

This duskily colored hybrid is free flowering and deservedly popular.

C. TRACYANUM

HEIGHT 36 in (90 cm)
SPREAD 36 in (90 cm)
FLOWERING Fall
TEMPERATURE Above 50°F (10°C)

This epiphytic species is native to Burma, Thailand, and China, where it grows on damp rocks and tree trunks at elevations of 4,000–6,200 ft (1,200–1,900 m). It has roughly oval pseudobulbs and arching, narrow, strappy leaves, 24–30 in (60–75 cm) long. The strongly fragrant, yellow-green flowers, 3½ in (9 cm) across, are held on arching spikes. Boldly striped with brown, the flowers have cream or yellow lips, flecked with purple-brown. Grow in a large pot filled with standard orchid potting mix.

This fascinating species can withstand exposure to near-freezing temperatures.

DENDROBIUM

Increasingly popular as houseplants, dendrobiums look quite different from many other orchids, distinguished by their tall cane-like pseudobulbs. Out of flower, they could almost be mistaken for miniature bamboos. Several are ideal for growing on a **windowsill and their showy, vividly colored flowers make them popular with florists. The star of the genus was for a long time *Dendrobium nobile*, along with plants derived from it, but that situation looks likely to change with the introduction of new hybrids.**

ABOUT THESE PLANTS

This large, variable genus comprises more than 900 species of evergreen and deciduous sympodial orchids that grow both epiphytically and on the ground, sometimes on rocks. They are distributed widely across the tropics, growing from India and southeast Asia to New Guinea, Australia, and the Pacific Islands. Dendrobiums grow in rainforests from low altitudes up to mountain forests more than 7,000 ft (2,000 m) above sea level.

Pseudobulbs are usually upright and stemlike and are set with relatively small leaves, sometimes at the tips, with a bare length of stem behind them. The showy flowers are produced on short stalks that emerge from the leaf bases or are held in generous clusters. Such is the diversity shown by the genus that some botanists have attempted to split it into several smaller groups, but these have not generally been accepted. Some species were used in traditional Chinese medicine and the bulbous stems of the Australian *Dendrobium canaliculatum* were used as a food by indigenous peoples.

HOW TO GROW

Dendrobiums are cool growing orchids, needing a winter minimum temperature of 50°F (10°C) and a summer maximum of 60°–70°F (16–21°C). Grow them in small pots filled with

epiphytic orchid potting mix. The plants tend to be tall and need help to prevent them keeling over. Grow them in heavy pots, or weight the base of your pots with stones. Those with drooping canes are best displayed when attached to bark slabs.

From late spring to summer, keep plants partially shaded but move them to full light between fall and early spring. Water frequently in spring and summer, adding fertilizer at every third watering, and mist twice daily. Ventilate well to prevent stagnant conditions. Keep plants dry in winter, especially when temperatures fall. Stake the tall flowering stems of plants in pots.

REPOTTING AND PROPAGATION

Dendrobiums do not like to be disturbed so should be repotted only when the stems appear crowded in their pots. This applies to tall varieties, too, where there is a temptation to repot when they appear top-heavy. Repot when dormant in winter or just as growth is beginning in spring. Both deciduous and evergreen types can be divided. Deciduous types can also be increased by stem cuttings from older stems that are bare toward the base. Each cutting should have at least one or two dormant buds (see p.45).

SA-NOOK HYBRIDS

Developed by Suphachadiwong Orchids in Thailand, Sa-nook® varieties of dendrobium have been carefully selected for their vigor and ability to flower freely in typical living room conditions. They are tolerant of higher temperatures and drier atmospheres than many other dendrobiums. The flowers are typically large and richly colored with a plush texture, and some varieties are known to bloom for 12 weeks or more. Future developments are expected to increase the flower size and color range still further.

Sa-nook Purple Happiness is a colorful, fast-growing variety.

Dendrobiums can be propagated from cuttings from older canes (see p.45).

D. APHYLLUM

HEIGHT 3 ft (1 m)
SPREAD 6 in (15 cm)
FLOWERING Spring
TEMPERATURE Above 50°F (10°C)

These trailing orchids are found in the Himalaya and from southwest China to Malaysia, where they grow in wet tropical conditions, often among rocks. They have pendent pseudobulbs and slender, narrow, fleshy leaves to 4¾ in (12 cm) long. The flowers, 2 in (5 cm) across, are pale mauve pink and have cone-shaped lips, giving rise to the plant's common name of "hooded orchid." The plant is best grown on a bark slab, suspended at eye level, from which flowers can cascade.

The generous, delicately colored flowers are carried in pairs.

D. BERRY 'ODA'

HEIGHT 14 in (35 cm)
SPREAD 8 in (20 cm)
FLOWERING Spring to mid-summer
TEMPERATURE Above 50°F (10°C)

With upright, cane-like pseudobulbs, this compact hybrid produces masses of lightly scented flowers with mauve-pink petals that fade to white toward the center. It was created by crossing the Australian species D. kingianum with D. Mini Pearl. The leathery, pointed leaves, are up to 4 in (10 cm) long. Well-grown plants are dense and impressive when in full flower; their berrylike scent is most noticeable in the morning and again at dusk. Grow in small pots filled with standard orchid potting mix.

This orchid is a winner, producing an abundance of long-lasting flowers.

D. CHRYSANTHUM

HEIGHT 3–6 ft (1–2 m)
SPREAD 18 in (45 cm)
FLOWERING Spring (usually)–fall
TEMPERATURE Above 50°F (10°C)

This plant is found from the eastern Himalaya to Burma and Thailand, where it grows in humid forests at altitudes of 1,150–7,200 ft (350–2,200 m). It has pendent, cane-like pseudobulbs, 3–6 ft (1–2 m) long, with lance-shaped leaves, 4–8 in (10–20 cm) long, along their lengths. The fragrant, fleshy flowers, 1½ in (4 cm) across, are bright golden yellow and can appear at any time during the growing season. Grow in a sturdy wire or wooden basket that can accommodate the plant's bulk.

The yellow flower lips usually have two chestnut brown spots at their base.

D. HAPPINESS

HEIGHT 2 ft (60 cm)
SPREAD 10 in (25 cm)
FLOWERING Spring
TEMPERATURE Above 50°F (10°C)

This hybrid, produced by crossing D. Kobayashi with D. Misstomopink, has fleshy, mainly pendent or outward-facing, cane-like pseudobulbs that are sometimes kinked or curved. The glossy, lance-shaped leaves are 4 in (10 cm) long. Creamy white flowers, 1½ in (4 cm) across, are produced singly or in pairs and have lips that are heavily blotched with deep chestnut brown toward the base. It is best grown attached to an upright slab of bark suspended at eye level, with roots always exposed to the air.

The flowers of this orchid hang downward on unusually long stalks.

Deservedly popular, Berry 'Oda' is one of the easiest dendrobiums to grow.

D. INFUNDIBULUM

HEIGHT 24 in (60 cm)
SPREAD 6 in (15 cm)
FLOWERING Spring–summer
TEMPERATURE Above 50°F (10°C)

This orchid is from Burma and Thailand, where it grows in dense forests at altitudes of 650–7,545 ft (200–2,300 m). The pseudobulbs are slender and erect, bearing narrow, dark green leaves, to 4¾ in (12 cm) long, on their upper parts. The sheath at the base of each leaf is covered in black hairs. The long-lasting, translucent white flowers, 3 in (8 cm) across, have a round, yellow or orange spot at the base of each lip. Plants may shed their leaves in winter. Grow these plants in small pots or baskets filled with standard orchid potting mix.

The long-lasting funnel-lipped flowers are produced in pairs on the cane-like stems.

D. 'IRENE SMILE'

HEIGHT 18–24 in (45–60 cm)
SPREAD 8–10 in (20–25 cm)
FLOWERING Spring
TEMPERATURE Above 50°F (10°C)

This hybrid is a good choice to start your dendrobium collection. It has well-scented flowers generously clustered on upright, cane-like pseudobulbs. The blooms, some 2 in (5 cm) across, are white, marked with dark pink toward the tips of the petals and lips. Each lip has a pale yellow-green center. The narrowly oval leaves are bright green and 3–4 in (8–10 cm) long. Flowering can occur beyond the typical spring season. Grow in small pots or baskets filled with standard orchid potting mix.

Delicate markings toward the edges of the flower give this hybrid a unique appeal.

D. KINGIANUM

HEIGHT 6 in (15 cm)
SPREAD 6 in (15 cm)
FLOWERING Spring
TEMPERATURE Above 55°F (13°C)

This variable species is from eastern Australia, where it typically grows among rocks in open forests or near creeks. It has narrowly conical pseudobulbs, 2–10 in (5–30 cm) long and narrowly oval leaves, 1–4 in (3–10 cm) long, that emerge near the tip of the pseudobulb. Up to 15 fragrant, pink, purple, or white flowers, with diameters of up to 1½ in (4 cm), are produced in loose clusters around 6 in (15 cm) in length. Grow this plant in small pots or baskets filled with standard orchid potting mix.

With its delicate flowers, this robust species is one of the easiest dendrobiums to grow.

D. MACROPHYLLUM

HEIGHT 36 in (90 cm)
SPREAD 12 in (30 cm)
FLOWERING Spring–summer
TEMPERATURE Above 55°F (13°C)

Native to Indonesia, the Philippines, and New Guinea, this easy growing plant, sometimes known as "pastor's orchid," occurs naturally in forests from sea level to 5,575 ft (1,700 m). It has club- or spindle-shaped pseudobulbs and its oblong leaves are 6–12 in (15–30 cm) long. The scented flowers, 2 in (5 cm) across, are yellow to yellowish green, conspicuously spotted and striped with purple in the lips, the stripes forking toward the margins. Grow in pots or baskets filled with standard orchid potting mix; avoid repotting until absolutely necessary.

Flowers are long-lasting, intriguingly patterned, and lightly fragrant.

D. MOMOZONO 'PRINCESS'

HEIGHT 24 in (60 cm)
SPREAD 12 in (30 cm)
FLOWERING Spring
TEMPERATURE Above 50°F (10°C)

This eye-catching orchid is a hybrid of *D.* Angel Flower and *D.* Glorious Rainbow. It produces oblong leaves, some 4 in (10 cm) long, on upright, cane-like pseudobulbs, and its flowers are densely clustered in pairs toward the tips of the pseudobulbs. Some 2¾ in (7 cm) across, the blooms are dark pink, fading to white at the center. Lips are blotchy in the throat—a bright yellow edged with white—and pink at the margins. Grow in pots or baskets filled with standard orchid potting mix.

Flowers of this cultivar are extremely eye-catching and dense, overlapping one another other on stemlike pseudobulbs.

D. NOBILE

HEIGHT 18 in (45 cm)
SPREAD 6 in (15 cm)
FLOWERING Spring
TEMPERATURE Above 50°F (10°C)

Widely used in breeding programs to create new cultivars, this species is found in the Himalaya and southern China, in both lowland and mountain forests. It has upright, cane-like pseudobulbs and lance-shaped leaves, to 4¾ in (12 cm) long. Scented flowers, 2½ in (6 cm) across, are pale rose-pink, darkening toward the margins and white toward the base, with a dark maroon blotch on each lip. It sometimes loses its leaves over winter. Grow in medium to large pots filled with standard orchid potting mix.

Many dendrobium hybrids available in the orchid trade can trace their parentage back to this species.

D. ORIENTAL PARADISE

HEIGHT 24 in (60 cm)
SPREAD 12 in (30 cm)
FLOWERING Spring
TEMPERATURE Above 50°F (10°C)

A hybrid of *D.* Evening Glow and *D.* Oborozuki, this orchid has upright, cane-like pseudobulbs set with narrow, oblong, dark green leaves, 4 in (10 cm) long, that extend beyond the flower clusters. Lower portions of the pseudobulbs are often leafless. White flowers, 2¾ in (7 cm) across, have dark pink notches at the tips of the petals and are held tight against the stem; the lips carry red blotches with yellow edges. Grow in small pots or baskets filled with standard orchid potting mix.

The pastel-colored flowers are produced in pairs.

D. 'POLAR FIRE'

HEIGHT 20 in (50 cm)
SPREAD 8 in (20 cm)
FLOWERING Winter–spring
TEMPERATURE Above 59°F (15°C)

This compact hybrid forms clumps of thick, cane-like pseudobulbs that carry lance-shaped, glossy, dark green leaves up to 4 in (10 cm) in length. Elegant sprays of flowers, carried on long, slender stems, emerge from the tips of the pseudobulbs. The sweetly scented blooms, 2 in (5 cm) across, are white, heavily suffused with rich purple, darkening toward the flower center and forming veins toward the petal edges. Grow in small pots or baskets filled with standard orchid potting mix.

This orchid is named for its distinctive colors, said to resemble those of the northern lights.

D. POLYSEMA

HEIGHT 36 in (90 cm)
SPREAD 28 in (70 cm)
FLOWERING Winter–spring
TEMPERATURE Above 59°F (15°C)

Native to Malaysia, New Guinea, the Solomon Islands, Fiji, and Samoa, this variable species is found in cloud forests at elevations of 4,000–6,350 ft (1,200–1,900 m). The club- to spindle-shaped pseudobulbs are 20 in (50 cm) long; from their tips emerge oblong leaves, 6–12 in (15–30 cm) long, and an erect branching flower spike. The fragrant flowers, to 2½ in (6 cm) across, are yellow or yellow-green, with purple stripes or spots on the lips. Grow in small pots filled with standard orchid potting mix.

The outer surfaces of the flowers are densely hairy.

D. SA-NOOK BLUE HAPPINESS

HEIGHT 18–28 in (45–70 cm)
SPREAD 8 in (20 cm)
FLOWERING Fall–winter
TEMPERATURE Above 59°F (15°C)

One of a group of hybrids bred to thrive in modern, centrally heated living rooms, Blue Happiness has erect, cane-like pseudobulbs that are set with lance-shaped, bright green leaves, to 4 in (10 cm) long. The flowers, 1½–1¾ in (3–4 cm) across, are carried in clusters on a single stem that emerges from the tip of each pseudobulb. They are deep purplish-blue, fading to white toward the center, where some veining may be present. Grow these plants in small pots filled with standard orchid potting mix.

This hybrid flourishes in the warm conditions of our modern homes.

D. SA-NOOK PURPLE HAPPINESS

HEIGHT 18–28 in (45–70 cm)
SPREAD 8 in (20 cm)
FLOWERING Fall–winter
TEMPERATURE Above 59°F (15°C)

As with other Sa-Nook hybrids, this orchid makes an ideal houseplant because it tolerates typical living room conditions. Pseudobulbs are upright and cane-like, bearing lance-shaped leaves, to 4 in (10 cm) long. The flowers, 1½–1¾ in (3–4 cm) across, are carried in clusters on a single stem that emerges from the tip of the pseudobulb, and are rich crimson-purple with white centers. Given appropriate care, the flowering period can extend to eight weeks. Grow in small pots filled with standard orchid potting mix.

With its vibrant flowers, this is one of the most eye-catching of the newer orchid hybrids.

D. SPIRAL GEM 'UNIVERSAL TOPAZ'

HEIGHT 10–14 in (25–35 cm)
SPREAD 3 ft (1 m)
FLOWERING Winter–spring
TEMPERATURE Above 50°F (10°C)

The result of a cross between D. Salak and the species D. canaliculatum from tropical North Queensland and New Guinea, this orchid has cane-like pseudobulbs and narrowly oval leaves, 4–10 in (10–25 cm) long. The flowers, ⅜–½ in (8–12 mm) across, are carried in groups of six to nine on airy flowering spikes, 12 in (30 cm) long. Twisting petals are greenish yellow, fading to white toward the base. Grow in small pots filled with orchid potting mix and leave plants undisturbed as much as possible.

The flowers have a spiderlike appearance and prominently red-marked lips.

D. SPRING DREAM 'APOLLON'

HEIGHT 24 in (60 cm)
SPREAD 10 in (25 cm)
FLOWERING Spring–summer
TEMPERATURE Above 50°F (10°C)

A hybrid of D. Constance Wrigley and D. Thwaitesiae, this plant has fleshy, cane-like pseudobulbs. From their upper halves emerge oval, glossy green leaves, to 3 in (8 cm) long. Short flowering spikes from the nodes carry slightly fragrant, pure white flowers, 2½ in (7 cm) across, with yellowish green centers. This plant, impressive when in full flower, is widely available and popular for its ease of cultivation. Flowering can sometimes begin in winter. Grow in a small pot filled with standard orchid potting mix.

Plentiful flowers cover the upper part, or sometimes the whole length, of the pseudobulb.

D. VICTORIAE-REGINAE

HEIGHT 24 in (60 cm)
SPREAD 10 in (25 cm)
FLOWERING Usually spring, but also at other times
TEMPERATURE Above 50°F (10°C)

This species from the Philippines grows on moss-covered trees at altitudes of 4,265–8,850 ft (1,300–2,700 m). The narrowly cylindrical pseudobulbs, 10–24 in (25–60 cm) long, hang downward, and are set with papery, oblong leaves, 1¼–3¼ in (3–8 cm) long. Flowers, 1¼ in (3 cm) across, are bright violet-blue with white bases and are carried on short spikes of one to three. Grow this orchid attached to a bark slab or in a slatted basket from which the flowers can cascade.

The flowers seem almost luminous; they can appear at virtually any time of year.

D. WILLIAMSONII

HEIGHT 16 in (40 cm)
SPREAD 10 in (25 cm)
FLOWERING Late winter–early spring
TEMPERATURE Above 50°F (10°C)

Native to southern China, Assam, and Indochina, this compact orchid is found in forests at elevations of 1,950–4,600 ft (600–1,400 m). The upright pseudobulbs are velvety, as are the lance-shaped leaves, to 4 in (10 cm) long. The waxy, cream or yellow flowers, to 3 in (7.5 cm) across, have a strongly spicy or citrusy fragrance. The lips, finely toothed or fringed at the margin, are marked with a large red or brown blotch. Grow in small to medium pots filled with standard orchid potting mix.

Flowers are produced singly or in pairs on stout, densely clustered pseudobulbs.

D. Spring Dream 'Apollon' is widely grown and admired for its dense floral displays.

DRACULA

This genus has a somewhat sinister name and does indeed contain some striking plants that will appeal to lovers of the gothic. The name was applied to the genus because of the blood-red flower color of several of its species and the bizarre appearance of the long spurs, or tails, at the tips of their sepals. Other members of this genus have prominent, face-like markings at the center of their flowers, giving them an uncanny anthropomorphic quality. Draculas make excellent subjects for hanging baskets in an unheated conservatory or greenhouse.

Dracula gigas, a native of Colombia and Ecuador, is commonly known as the monkey orchid for obvious reason.

Dracula orchids have distinctive elongated tails that only add to their eerie attraction.

ABOUT THESE PLANTS

Dracula is a genus of evergreen epiphytes from the Andean regions of South America and mountainous parts of Central America; almost half originate in Ecuador. These plants lack pseudobulbs, instead producing short, slender stems along a creeping rhizome. Each stem has a single, dark green, folded leaf, with a sharply defined mid-rib. The leaves are often spongy in texture, fulfilling the function of pseudobulbs as water-storage organs. Usually arching stems carry either a single flower or several in a cluster. The stems emerge horizontally from the base of the plant or hang down. The sepals of the flowers, which end in long "tails," are fused in a cuplike arrangement, the petals being much smaller and thicker. The lips are often large and mushroomlike—adaptations to attract flies, their pollinators.

HOW TO GROW

Draculas are cool growing, needing a winter minimum temperature of 50°F (10°C) with a summer maximum of 75°F (24°C). Keep them in a cool, shady, well-ventilated area, where roots will remain damp. Add sphagnum moss or an equivalent to epiphytic potting mix to help retain moisture. Water freely in spring and summer, making sure they drain fully after watering; excessively wet potting mix can cause root rot. Apply fertilizer at every third watering; use a high-nitrogen feed in spring and summer, switching to high-potassium in late summer and fall. Water more sparingly in winter, though plants should not be allowed to dry out completely. Allow flowers to fade on the stems until they are shed naturally — the stems may produce further flower buds.

REPOTTING AND PROPAGATION

Repot plants when they fill the container or basket, usually every two to three years. Congested plants can also be divided at the same time, using a sharp knife to sever the rhizome between the stems.

D. BELLA

HEIGHT 10in (25cm)
SPREAD 10in (25cm)
FLOWERING Winter–summer
TEMPERATURE Above 50°F (10°C)

This species is native to Colombia and Ecuador, where it grows in dense cloud forests at altitudes of 5,580–6,500ft (1,700–2,000m). It has roughly oblong leaves that reach lengths of 4¾–8in (12–20cm) and nodding, long-tailed, fragrant flowers up to 10–25cm (4–10in) long. These blooms are produced singly; they are greenish yellow and heavily spotted with brown. The lips are small and white. Grow in a slatted basket filled with standard orchid potting mix.

The triangular flowers have a central "face" and are produced around the base of the plant.

D. VAMPIRA

HEIGHT 16in (40cm)
SPREAD 20in (50cm)
FLOWERING Any time
TEMPERATURE Above 50°F (10°C)

This species occurs exclusively in Ecuador, on the slopes of Mount Pichincha, where it grows in abundance at altitudes of 6,250–7,200ft (1,900–2,200m). Its erect, bladelike leaves are 6–11in (15–28cm) long. Flowers, to 10in (25cm) in length, are green but covered with blackish purple veins that merge toward the center; the tails are almost completely black. The lips are white, marked with pinkish veins. Grow in a slatted basket filled with standard orchid potting mix.

This species produces the darkest-colored flowers of any of the draculas.

DENDROCHILUM GLUMACEUM

HEIGHT 12in (30cm)
SPREAD 8in (20cm)

FLOWERING Winter
TEMPERATURE Above 55°F (13°C)

With small flowers densely packed on the spike, this orchid looks quite unlike most others.

Dendrochilum is a genus of evergreen, epiphytic orchids from southeast Asia and New Guinea. Plants grow in rather exposed conditions at altitudes of 2,300–7,000ft (700–2,000m). There are more than 300 species, but only a few are available commercially, of which *D. glumaceum* is the most widely grown. This is a sympodial species from the Philippines that forms a clump of roughly oval pseudobulbs, each of which produces a single narrow leaf measuring around 12in (30cm) in length. Its sweetly scented, star-shaped, white flowers, are up to ¾in (2cm) across, but never open fully. They are carried densely in two rows in tapering, arching clusters on a spike that emerges from the center of the plant, extending to a length of 16in (40cm).

HOW TO GROW This is an intermediate-growing orchid, needing a winter minimum temperature of 55°F (13°C) and a summer maximum of 80°F (30°C). Like all dendrochilums it should be grown in a well-ventilated location in a small to medium pot filled with standard orchid potting mix.

This orchid grows in winter and rests in summer. Water weekly when in growth, allowing plants to dry out between waterings. Add fertilizer at every third watering (high nitrogen in winter, high potassium in spring). Keep plants in good light but screen them from hot sun in summer. Repot or divide plants, if necessary, in spring after flowering. You can also propagate by cutting off dormant back bulbs and potting them up separately.

EPIDENDRUM

This large genus contains some 750 species, but only a few are available commercially and of interest to orchid growers. They range in size from small, tufted plants no more than 6 in (15 cm) high to tall reedlike orchids that can top 6 ft (2 m). The genus name makes reference to the epiphytic habit, though in practice, not all species grow epiphytically. When the genus was named by Carl Linnaeus in 1763, he included in it all the orchids known at the time that grew epiphytically. While some members of the genus have very specific needs, several are suitable for growing at home.

ABOUT THESE PLANTS

These varied orchids are widespread in tropical North, Central, and South America. Depending on species, they may be epiphytic, lithophytic, or terrestrial. Many do not produce pseudobulbs but have cylindrical, leafy stems that can be tall and reedlike or short and fleshy. Leaf shape varies considerably. Flowers are small but are usually produced in clusters and can be fragrant. They tend to open in succession, a few at a time, so plants may be in flower for several months.

HOW TO GROW

Epidendrums are cool to intermediate growing, needing a winter minimum temperature of 50–55°F (10–13°C). Summer temperatures should not exceed 86°F (30°C) for all types. In spring and summer, keep plants in a bright position screened from strong sun. Water freely, applying fertilizer at every third watering. High humidity is important, so mist once or twice daily. Place plants in full light in winter and reduce watering. Types with pseudobulbs can be kept dry in winter. Terra-cotta pots that provide ballast are most appropriate for large plants that may also need stem support. Small epidendrums are suitable for growing in baskets or mounted on bark.

Epidendrum piliferum has a profusion of apple-green, white lipped flowers.

REPOTTING AND PROPAGATION

Repot these orchids when they grow so tall and top-heavy as to be unstable in their existing pots or when the potting mix develops a crusty appearance: this is usually every two to three years. Congested plants can be divided at the same time, using a sharp knife to cut them into sections. Some plants produce roots from the stem toward the stem tip. If the roots are well developed, sever the stem just below the roots using sharp pruners and pot up the plantlet in the appropriate potting mix for growing on.

E. DIFFORME

HEIGHT 14 in (35 cm)
SPREAD 12 in (30 cm)
FLOWERING Summer (mainly)
TEMPERATURE Above 55°F (13°C)

This epiphytic species is found at elevations of up to 5,000 ft (1,500 m) in the wet tropical areas of Florida, Mexico, Central America, and northern parts of South America. Its has flattened stems and narrow, fleshy or leathery, glossy, yellow-green leaves, to 4½ in (11 cm) long. The greenish yellow or white, almost translucent flowers are 1¼ in (3 cm) across and are carried in clusters up to 6 in (15 cm) across. Grow in medium pots filled with standard orchid potting mix.

The pale, medicinally scented, flowers can emerge at almost any time of year.

E. × OBRIENIANUM

HEIGHT 3 ft (1 m)
SPREAD 3 ft (1 m)
FLOWERING Any time
TEMPERATURE Above 50°F (10°C)

This epiphytic orchid is a hybrid of E. ibaguense, from Central and South America, and E. jamiesonis, from Colombia and Ecuador. It has tall, rambling, leafy stems and roughly oval, yellowish-green leaves, up to 6 in (15 cm) long. The orange to bright orange-red flowers are 1½ in (4 cm) across, long lasting, and produced in clusters. In ideal growing conditions, these plants can flower more or less continuously. Grow in large pots filled with standard orchid potting mix or attached to bark slabs.

This orchid is capable of producing a seemingly unending succession of vivid flowers.

E. PLASTIC DOLL

HEIGHT 36 in (90 cm)
SPREAD 24 in (60 cm)
FLOWERING Summer–fall
TEMPERATURE Above 55°F (13°C)

This orchid is a hybrid between E. pseudepidendrum and E. ilense. Its stems are generously set with leathery, glossy, mid-green leaves, each up to 8 in (20 cm) long. Gleaming, fleshy, bright green flowers, 2 in (5 cm) long, have protruding, bright orange lips with finely fringed lobes. They may be produced several times in one season in loose clusters up to 6 in (15 cm) long at the ends of long, drooping stems. Grow this orchid in a medium to large pot filled with standard orchid potting mix.

The flowers of Plastic Doll are uniquely shiny; the lip has a glossy finish.

E. RADICANS

HEIGHT 4½ ft (1.3 m)
SPREAD 12 in (30 cm)
FLOWERING Any time
TEMPERATURE Above 55°F (13°C)

This terrestrial species hails from the West Indies, Mexico, Central America, and parts of South America. It often grows in open areas and on roadside banks. Tall, upright, leafy stems are set with roughly oblong, leathery, yellowish green leaves, 6 in (15 cm) long. Bright red or occasionally orange or yellow flowers, 1½ in (4 cm) across, are produced in dense clusters. Grow it in medium to large containers filled with terrestrial orchid potting mix. Larger plants can become perpetually blooming, so divide only when necessary.

Intensely colored flowers give this plant its informal name, "fire-star orchid."

LAELIA

Named after one of the Vestal Virgins—priestesses of ancient Rome—laelias are related to cattleyas and are used in breeding programs with them to create glamorous hybrids. They could easily be mistaken for cattleyas, but the flowers tend to be smaller and more brightly colored, making them ideal for corsages or flamboyant buttonholes. Many are robust, becoming substantial, clustering plants in only a few years, so are ideal for amateur growers with the space to accommodate them. Small types make ideal windowsill plants.

Laelia orchids generally bloom in the fall or winter seasons.

Laelia **Splendid Spire 'Rose Midnight'** demonstrates the vibrant lips of this genus.

ABOUT THESE PLANTS

The genus *Laelia* comprises some 25 species of evergreen sympodial orchids. They grow from Mexico to Brazil and Bolivia up to altitudes of 8,200 ft (2,600 m), often in oak woods. They have robust but often slender pseudobulbs from which one to three rather rigid leaves emerge. Pseudobulbs are spaced on a horizontal rhizome that will rapidly creep over the edges of any pot. Flowering spikes appear from the tips of mature pseudobulbs.

The petals and sepals are often widely spaced and narrower than those of the cattleyas, while the lip is often the most striking part of the flower, trumpetlike and ruffled at the outer edge.

HOW TO GROW

Laelias are cool growing, needing a winter minimum temperature of 50°F (10°C) with a summer maximum of 86°F (30°C). Keep them shaded in summer and mist once or twice daily to increase humidity. Water freely in spring and summer and add fertilizer at every third watering. Use a high-nitrogen fertilizer in spring and summer, then switch to a high-potassium feed in late summer to mature the growth and encourage flowering. Move plants to a position in full light in winter and water only to prevent them from drying out completely. Types with large flowers usually benefit from staking.

REPOTTING AND PROPAGATION

Laelias are fast growing and should be repotted once the pseudobulbs start to creep outside the pot. They need three or four pseudobulbs to flower successfully, so only larger plants should be divided; the best time for this is just after flowering. Cut the rhizome with a sharp knife between the pseudobulbs. Healthy dormant back bulbs can also be potted up separately.

L. ANCEPS

HEIGHT 18–24 in (45–60 cm)
SPREAD 12 in (30 cm)
FLOWERING Winter
TEMPERATURE Above 50°F (10°C)

This plant occurs in central Mexico in oak and pine forests (and also in coffee plantations) at altitudes of 1,650–5,000 ft (500–1,500 m). It has roughly oval, flat-sided pseudobulbs, each with one or two strappy, leathery leaves, around 6 in (15 cm) long. Spikes up to 24 in (60 cm) long carry two to five light rose-pink flowers, 2½ in (6 cm) across. The blooms have purple lips and yellow throats with purple veining. Grow in medium to large pots filled with standard orchid potting mix.

This winter-flowering species is a delightful choice for growing in the home.

L. AUTUMNALIS

HEIGHT 12–39 in (30–100 cm)
SPREAD 12 in (30 cm)
FLOWERING Winter
TEMPERATURE Above 50°F (10°C)

Originating in Mexico, this Laelia species grows epiphytically and on rocks at elevations of 5,000–8,500 ft (1,500–2,600 m). It has roughly egg-shaped pseudobulbs, each of which produces two or three narrowly oblong, leathery leaves, 4¾–8 in (12–20 cm) long. Its flowers are held in clusters of 4 to 10 on stems 12–39 in (30–100 cm) long. Measuring 2½ in (6 cm) across, they are rose-pink with rose-purple lips. Grow in medium to large pots filled with standard orchid potting mix.

Large, fragrant flowers make this a popular species with collectors.

This beautiful plant makes an excellent choice for a warm room.

LUDISIA DISCOLOR

HEIGHT 16–20 in (40–50 cm)
SPREAD 16–20 in (40–50 cm)

FLOWERING Spring
TEMPERATURE Above 59°F (15°C)

The genus Ludisia consists of a single species (or two, according to some taxonomists). L. discolor—sometimes known as the "jewel orchid"—is a terrestrial sympodial orchid that occurs naturally in a range of warm regions from the Himalaya to Java, where it grows on the forest floor.

This orchid has a creeping rhizome with no pseudobulbs. Succulent stems carry velvety, dark purple-brown leaves, 1½–2¼ in (4–7 cm) long, which are veined with red or gold. Flowers, up to ¾ in (2 cm) long, are borne on an 3¼ in (8 cm) stem; they are white with a yellow lip. Uniquely among the orchids, this plant is grown more for its foliage than for the flowers.

HOW TO GROW Ludisia discolor is warm growing, needing a minimum winter temperature of 59°F (15°C) and tolerating a maximum of 77°F (25°C) in summer. Grow it in a medium pot filled with terrestrial orchid potting mix. It favors indirect light; screen it from the sun in summer to protect the leaves from scorching. Water freely during spring and summer and apply fertilizer at every third watering. Water in winter only to prevent the potting mix from drying out. Plants can be potted on or divided; this is usually necessary every two or three years. Do this immediately after flowering using a sharp knife to cut through the rhizome.

LYCASTE

Among the largest of the commonly grown orchids, lycastes are valued for their generous free-flowering habit. Unlike many other orchids, they are very sensitive to high temperatures in summer, preferring cooler conditions. Regular feeding in spring and summer and a good winter rest seem to suit them well. Several species are widely available, and numerous hybrids have been derived from them, some through interbreeding with the related *Anguloa* (to produce *Angulocaste*). If space is limited, look to the more compact types, which can make excellent house plants.

ABOUT THESE PLANTS

Lycastes naturally grow as epiphytes and on the ground in the cloud forests of Mexico, Central and South America, and the West Indies. They have robust, roughly oval pseudobulbs and broad, strappy leaves that are sometimes folded centrally along their length; the leaves are shed in winter. Flowers are produced singly on leafless stems that appear from the base of the plant. The sepals, sometimes attractively spotted, splay outward in a triangular formation while the smaller petals form a cup; the lips are divided into three lobes.

HOW TO GROW

These plants are cool growing, needing a winter minimum temperature of 52–54°F (11–12°C) with a summer maximum of 68°F (20°C). Epiphytes can be grown in standard orchid potting mix or on bark slabs, while terrestrial species need a finer growing medium. Water plants freely in summer, but keep the leaves dry; feed at every third watering using a high-nitrogen feed in spring and a high-potassium fertilizer in summer–fall. Misting is not necessary; to keep these orchids cool in summer, ventilate well and grow them in shade. Move them to a position in full light in winter and water only if the pseudobulbs show signs of shriveling.

Lycastes are natural woodlanders, needing cool, shady conditions to produce their often stunning flowers.

REPOTTING AND PROPAGATION

Repot in summer, after flowering, when the pseudobulbs have filled their pots. With adequate feeding and light, these orchids are vigorous and can rapidly outgrow their containers. Depending on the vigor of your plant, this may make repotting necessary every year or every other year. The plants can be divided at the same time, and dormant back bulbs can be removed for growing on separately. This practice will result in manageably sized plants; to produce a larger, more impressive specimen, repot the plant without dividing.

L. AROMATICA

HEIGHT 12 in (30 cm)
SPREAD 12 in (30 cm)
FLOWERING Spring–summer
TEMPERATURE Above 52°F (11°C)

This species grows naturally on damp ground or sometimes epiphytically in Mexico, Guatemala, Belize, and Honduras. It has narrow leaves that reach lengths of 12–16 in (30–40 cm). Its cinnamon-scented flowers are some 1½–2½ in (4–6 cm) across, and are produced in abundance. They have deep golden to orange-yellow petals, yellowish green sepals, and lips dotted with orange. Grow in medium pots filled with terrestrial orchid potting mix or a mixture of fine bark and perlite.

The waxy flowers are sweetly scented, as the botanical name suggests.

L. CRUENTA

HEIGHT 18 in (45 cm)
SPREAD 18 in (45 cm)
FLOWERING Spring–summer
TEMPERATURE Above 52°F (11°C)

This epiphytic species grows naturally in Mexico, Guatemala, El Salvador, and Costa Rica. Its narrow leaves reach lengths of about 18 in (45 cm). The freely produced flowers have a diameter of around 2¾ in (7 cm), and are faintly cinnamon scented. They have greenish-yellow sepals and yellowish-orange petals that are spotted with red near their bases. Lips are orange with red spots and patches at their bases. Grow in large pots filled with standard orchid potting mix or attached to a bark slab.

Flowers release their cinnamon fragrance mainly in the evening.

L. DEPPEI

HEIGHT 12 in (30 cm)
SPREAD 12 in (30 cm)
FLOWERING Spring–summer
TEMPERATURE Above 52°F (11°C)

Found in Mexico and Guatemala, this epiphytic species has lance-shaped leaves that reach lengths of 12–20 in (30–50 cm). The flowers, which are some 3½ in (9 cm) across, have green sepals spotted with red-brown; these contrast with white petals flecked with red-brown toward the base, and deep yellow lips that are spotted with red, and striped with red at the base. Carried on short stems, they cluster at the base of the plant. Grow in medium pots filled with standard orchid potting mix or attached to a bark slab.

Beautifully marked flowers are held singly on stems; they are produced in abundance on a well-grown plant.

MASDEVALLIA

These plants are tricky to grow but are among the most intriguing of all orchids. Their flowers often have brilliant, almost unnatural, colors and display flamboyant tail-like extensions to the spreading, triangular sepals. These tails have given the plants the common name "kite orchids." Properly cared for, masdevallias are desirable additions to any orchid collection and their compact size makes them easy to accommodate. While this is one of the largest orchid genera, only a few species are grown, alongside a small number of hybrids.

Distinctive, elongated tails are the defining characteristic of these fascinating orchids.

Masdevallia **Southern Sun** is aptly named, producing vivid tangerine-colored flowers.

ABOUT THESE PLANTS

Masdevallias are found from Mexico to southern Brazil, but the majority occur in the Andes at altitudes of 8,000–13,000 ft (2,500–4,000 m), where conditions are predominantly cool and misty. They can grow epiphytically, terrestrially, or on rocks as lithophytes. They form creeping rhizomes but have no pseudobulbs, which makes them sensitive to overly dry conditions in cultivation. Single-leaved, short stems grow from the rhizomes, carrying leaves that are roughly oval to elongated and mid- to dark green. The flowers, which vary in size and shape, are carried on spikes that emerge from the base of the plant. They are produced either singly or in clusters of several per stem. The distinctive tails greatly increase the overall size of the flower. Flowers of *M. macrura*, for example, can measure up to 12 in (30 cm) from top to bottom.

HOW TO GROW

These cool growing orchids need a minimum winter temperature of 52°F (11°C), and a summer maximum of 75°F (24°C). Daytime temperatures above 80°F (26°C) should be avoided. Grow them in well-ventilated, shaded sites in a fine-grade orchid potting mix; their delicate roots should not be exposed to the air, hence they are unsuitable for growing on bark. Masdevallias do not experience a resting period, so should be watered throughout the year, while avoiding over-wetting the potting mix.

REPOTTING AND PROPAGATION

Repot regularly, since the finer potting mix that these plants need will degrade rapidly. Repot in winter or early spring or just as new roots are starting to form. Make sure the newest growth is farthest from the rim of the container, unless new growth is appearing from around the perimeter, in which case the plants should be placed centrally. With no pseudobulbs, these plants are unsuitable for division, but offsets around the base of the plant may sometimes be removed for growing on.

M. BARLAEANA

HEIGHT 7 in (18 cm)
SPREAD 6 in (15 cm)
FLOWERING Summer–fall
TEMPERATURE Above 52°F (11°C)

This dense-growing orchid is naturally found on exposed, rocky slopes in Colombia, Ecuador, and Peru, at elevations of 7,200–10,150 ft (2,200–3,100 m). It produces narrow, strappy leaves, to 5 in (12.5 cm) long. The flowers, which are borne on slender, upright stems around 10 in (25 cm) long are produced singly. Around 1¼ in (3 cm) across, they are bright pinkish-red with darker stripes and have deep pinkish-red tails. Grow this plant in a small pot with fine grade orchid potting mix.

The near-luminous flowers can sometimes be produced in winter.

M. INFRACTA

HEIGHT 6 in (15 cm)
SPREAD 6 in (15 cm)
FLOWERING Summer
TEMPERATURE Above 52°F (11°C)

This native of Brazil, Peru, and Bolivia grows in mountain forests at altitudes of 3,500–6,500 ft (1,100–2,000 m). It has narrow, upright leaves that may reach lengths of 5½ in (14 cm). It produces between one and five flowers, which are 4–6 in (10–15 cm) across and are somewhat cupped and rounded in shape. The blooms are dull red to pinkish purple, flushed with yellow. Tails are long and pale yellow. Grow in small pots filled with fine grade orchid potting mix.

Unlike other *Masdevallia* species, the flowers do not open flat.

M. TOVARENSIS

HEIGHT 6 in (15 cm)
SPREAD 6 in (15 cm)
FLOWERING Winter
TEMPERATURE Above 52°F (11°C)

This species is found only in Venezuela, where it grows at elevations of 5,250–7,850 ft (1,600–2,400 m). It has upright to arching, bright glossy green leaves, which may reach lengths of up to 6 in (15 cm). The white flowers are 3 in (8 cm) long with relatively short tails; they appear in pairs or clusters of up to four, often overlapping, blooms. Do not cut stems back after flowering as plants may produce a second flush of blooms. Grow in small pots filled with fine grade orchid potting mix.

The wavy blooms are long lived on the plant, which often flowers in mid-winter.

M. WAGNERIANA

HEIGHT 5 in (12 cm)
SPREAD 5 in (12 cm)
FLOWERING Spring–fall
TEMPERATURE Above 52°F (11°C)

This species is found from Colombia to northern Venezuela at elevations of 3,600–6,000 ft (1,100–1,800 m). Its spatula-shaped leaves are up to 2 in (5 cm) long. Flowers, which are around 2¼ in (6 cm) across, are carried singly on short, slender stems. They are light green-yellow to cream, darkening to orange-yellow toward the base, and spotted and streaked with violet. The slender, curving tails are up to 2 in (5 cm) long. Grow in small pots filled with fine grade orchid potting mix.

The long-tailed flowers are distinctively and very generously spotted.

MAXILLARIA

The name of this genus is derived from the Latin word *maxilla*, meaning "jawbone," perhaps referring to the protruding lip seen in the flowers of some species. Several have found their way into the orchid trade and are available from specialist nurseries; others are too large and rampant for home growers but can be seen in botanic gardens. A number are prized for their sweet fragrance.

Maxillaria ochroleuca has strappy, pale yellow, well-scented flowers.

Many maxillaria species, including *M. tenuifolia* are more tolerant than other orchids and will grow in a broad range of conditions.

ABOUT THESE PLANTS

Maxillarias are epiphytic or terrestrial orchids found from central Mexico to Bolivia, also including the Caribbean. They are rainforest plants, growing from sea level to elevations of 11,500 ft (3,500 m), where temperatures can range from tropical to much cooler.

The pseudobulbs are rounded to oblong, clustered together on a short rhizome or more widely spaced on a longer one. Flowers are produced singly on stems growing from the base of the pseudobulbs. They are often small but a few species produce showier blooms. The lips can be hairy and have wartlike protuberances known as papillae.

HOW TO GROW

The maxillarias described here are all cool growing epiphytes, needing a minimum winter temperature of 50°F (10°C) and a summer maximum of 86°F (30°C); other species may need higher winter temperatures.

Grow these plants in pots or slatted baskets filled with standard orchid potting mix; smaller types are suitable for attaching to slabs of bark. For the best results, water plants freely in spring and summer and feed at every third watering, using a potassium-high fertilizer when the growth is maturing; this will help promote flowering. Mist plants once or twice daily. In fall and winter, water them just enough to keep the potting mix moist. Shade plants in summer but keep them in full light in winter.

REPOTTING AND PROPAGATION

Plants can be repotted once the new pseudobulbs have reached the rim of the container—usually every two to three years, but more often if growth is vigorous. They can be divided after flowering or propagated from dormant back bulbs. Alternatively, pot them on regularly without dividing to produce dense but free-flowering plants.

M. PORPHYROSTELE

HEIGHT 6 in (15 cm)
SPREAD 6 in (15 cm)
FLOWERING Winter–spring
TEMPERATURE Above 50°F (10°C)

This species grows naturally in forested regions of Brazil. It has clustering, roughly oval pseudobulbs, each with two narrow leaves, 8 in (20 cm) long. Its slightly fragrant, pale yellow flowers, 1 in (2.5 cm) across, are striped with purple in their throats. They are carried singly on short stems, to 3¼ in (8 cm) long, amid or below the leaves. Grow in small pots or baskets with standard orchid potting mix, or attached to slabs of bark.

The sepals curve inward when the flower is fully open.

M. PRAESTANS

HEIGHT 20 in (50 cm)
SPREAD 20 in (50 cm)
FLOWERING Summer
TEMPERATURE Above 50°F (10°C)

This species originates from the humid mountain forests of Mexico and Central America. It has narrowly oval pseudobulbs, up to 3½ in (9 cm) long, each bearing a strappy leaf to 16 in (40 cm) long. The solitary, long-lasting, fragrant flowers, 2¼ in (6 cm) across, are yellow, spotted and striped with brown, and have blackish lips. Grow in medium pots filled with standard orchid potting mix.

The flowers of this species, are carried on slender stems to 5 in (12 cm) long.

M. VARIABILIS

HEIGHT 6 in (15 cm)
SPREAD 12 in (30 cm)
FLOWERING Any time
TEMPERATURE Above 50°F (10°C)

This species from Mexico and Central America grows on or beneath trees in humid forests at elevations of 1,650–8,200 ft (500–2,500 m). It produces clustering, roughly oval pseudobulbs, each of which bears a single, narrow, grass-green leaf at its tip. Slender flowering stems, to 2 in (5 cm) long, carry solitary, long-lasting flowers, to ⅗ in (1.5 cm) across. The blooms vary in color from pale yellow to dark red and the lips are marked with red. Grow in small pots filled with standard orchid potting mix or on a bark slab.

The botanical name of this species indicates that flower color is variable.

MILTONIA

All but one of the eight species of the genus *Miltonia* are native to Brazil. These orchids are noted for their large, long-lasting flowers, usually produced in generous numbers. A well-grown plant in full flower can be spectacular. They are straightforward to keep, making them deservedly popular with growers and widely available at garden centers and specialized nurseries.

Miltonia flavescens produces sprays of star-shaped, yellowish flowers.

ABOUT THESE PLANTS

Found in warm, moist forests in Brazil, these evergreen, epiphytic orchids grow at altitudes of 650–5,000 ft (200–1,500 m). The majority are from the mountainous area between São Paulo and Rio de Janeiro. In their native habitat, they are fast-growing and form large colonies. These orchids have oval to cylindrical pseudobulbs, which are evenly spaced along rhizomes; from each pseudobulb arise two strappy leaves. Flowering stems appear from the bases of the pseudobulbs at various times of the year, carrying clusters of star-shaped, often fragrant flowers.

HOW TO GROW

These orchids are intermediate growing, needing a winter minimum temperature of 55°F (13°C) with a summer maximum of 86°F (30°C). They do not experience a resting period, so should be kept moist throughout the year. However, overwatering can result in root rot, so allow the potting mix to dry out between waterings; mist the top growth once or twice daily to keep the plants adequately moist. Feed the plants at every third watering when they are in active growth. Keep them lightly shaded in summer and in full light in winter. Some can be grown on bark.

Some miltonias have a slightly messy sprawling habit.

REPOTTING AND PROPAGATION

Plants should be potted on when the new pseudobulbs have reached the rim of the pot. At this point, move them into slightly larger pots or baskets filled with standard orchid potting mix.

Repotting is usually necessary every two to three years but can be done more frequently if growth is vigorous. Repot after flowering, when new leaf shoots appear. Plants can be divided at the same time, using a sharp knife or pruners to cut through the rhizome. Firm, healthy, dormant back bulbs can be removed for growing on separately.

M. CLOWESII

HEIGHT 9 in (23 cm)
SPREAD 9 in (23 cm)
FLOWERING Fall
TEMPERATURE Above 55°F (13°C)

Hailing from mountainous parts of southeastern Brazil, this orchid has narrowly oval pseudobulbs around 3–4 in (7–10 cm) long, and narrow leaves that reach lengths of 12 in (30 cm). Three to seven starlike flowers, each 2 in (5 cm) across, are held on upright stems. Opening in succession, they are greenish yellow, with chestnut brown barring, and their white lips are generously marked with violet purple toward the base. Grow in small to medium pots filled with standard orchid potting mix.

The spidery flowers of this orchid have dramatically marked sepals and petals.

M. SPECTABILIS

HEIGHT 9 in (23 cm)
SPREAD 9 in (23 cm)
FLOWERING Summer
TEMPERATURE Above 55°F (13°C)

This compact orchid grows at altitudes of around 2,600 ft (800 m) in Brazil. It has a low, creeping habit, and produces elongated, yellow-tinged pseudobulbs and narrowly oblong leaves, 6 in (15 cm) in length. Its flowers, 3 in (8 cm) across, can be white, red, or purple and are held, singly or in pairs, close to the leaves on stems that are 8 in (20 cm) long. The red or purple lips have three yellow ridges at the base. Grow in medium pots filled with standard orchid potting mix or on a bark slab.

Flower color is variable in this species with numerous recognized varieties.

M. SUNSET

HEIGHT 20 in (50 cm)
SPREAD 8 in (20 cm)
FLOWERING Any time
TEMPERATURE Above 55°F (13°C)

This plant, bred from the species *M. regnellii* and M. Goodale Moir, has become one of the world's most popular orchids, and is sold in supermarkets in some countries. Sunset has flattened oval pseudobulbs and soft, arching, pale green leaves. The flowers, opening virtually flat, are 2 in (5 cm) across with pale yellow sepals and petals and large, delicately veined pink lips with a bright red flare at their base. They are carried on upright, branching stems, standing just above the foliage. Grow in medium pots or baskets filled with standard orchid potting mix.

The bright multihued flowers create an instant tropical feel in a room.

MILTONIOPSIS

These charming plants are often called "pansy orchids", because their flattened flowers, prominently marked with contrasting blotches and flares, so closely resemble those of the popular outdoor bedding plants. The showy blooms are long-lasting on the plant but unfortunately are not suitable for cutting. The species are rarely grown outside specialized collections, but the many hybrids are compact and deservedly popular as houseplants, on occasion flowering twice a year. Miltoniopsis are sometimes confused with miltonias, though the flowers are distinctly different.

Miltoniopsis flowers, large relative to the size of the plant, open flat to reveal their beautiful markings.

A collection of miltoniopsis plants has immediate appeal.

ABOUT THESE PLANTS

This genus comprises five species of sympodial orchids, from which many hybrids have been produced. In the wild, they grow epiphytically from 1,000–7,000 ft (300–2,000 m) in Central and South America. They have roughly oval, flattened pseudobulbs that are partially covered by narrow, pale grayish-green leaves. Large-lipped, fragrant flowers are carried on spikes that appear from the base of the pseudobulb. Each pseudobulb can produce two spikes, each bearing usually three to six flowers.

HOW TO GROW

Miltoniopsis are cool-growing, needing a winter minimum temperature of 52°F (11°C) with a summer maximum of 75°F (24°C). Keep plants shaded in summer and water regularly, but allow the potting mix to drain and dry out between waterings—the roots may rot if too wet. Feed at every third watering. Humidity is essential, so mist plants daily using a fine spray to avoid marking the leaves. Give plants full light in winter and water only enough to keep the roots barely moist.

REPOTTING AND PROPAGATION

Repot plants when the roots have filled the container and new pseudobulbs have reached the rim—usually every two to three years. Do this after flowering, when new leaf shoots are appearing. Plants can also be divided at the same time and dormant back bulbs removed for growing on separately.

M. ANJOU 'ST PATRICK'

HEIGHT 9 in (23 cm)
SPREAD 9 in (23 cm)
FLOWERING Summer (mainly)
TEMPERATURE Above 52°F (11°C)

This hybrid, produced from *M.* Hoggar and *M.* Piccadilly, is deservedly popular as a house plant. The pseudobulbs are roughly oval and leaves are narrow, to 8 in (20 cm) long. The flowers are deep red, with a prominent, irregularly flaring, white-edged mark toward the base of the lips, with further yellow markings toward the center. Each pseudobulb produces one or two flower spikes, each bearing two to four flowers. Grow in small pots filled with standard orchid potting mix.

The fragrant flowers can last around three weeks on the plant.

M. HERRALEXANDRE

HEIGHT 18 in (45 cm)
SPREAD 12 in (30 cm)
FLOWERING Summer
TEMPERATURE Above 52°F (11°C)

Produced by crossing *M.* Alexandre Dumas with *M.* Herrenhausen, this showy orchid has flattened oval pseudobulbs and soft, pale green leaves to 10 in (25 cm) long. Fragrant flowers, 3 in (8 cm) across, are produced on upright spikes. They are white with large, deep pinkish red blotches to the base of the petals. Lips are marked with yellow at the center, and have radiating yellow and red lines. Grow in small pots filled with standard orchid potting mix. This hybrid has been used in breeding programs.

Large flowers open almost flat to reveal their attractive markings.

M. HOUGUEMONT

HEIGHT 9 in (23 cm)
SPREAD 9 in (23 cm)
FLOWERING Summer
TEMPERATURE Above 52°F (11°C)

Produced by crossing *M.* Hautlieu with *M.* Leoville, this hybrid has roughly oval pseudobulbs and narrow leaves, to 8 in (20 cm) long. Its sweetly fragrant white flowers, to 3 in (8 cm) across, have a pinkish red blotch at the base of each petal, and radiating yellow lines and small central red areas on the lips. Like other members of the genus, this cultivar makes an excellent house plant. Grow in small pots filled with standard orchid potting mix and repot annually after flowering.

Up to six flowers per upright spike can be open at any one time.

M. PINK CADILLAC

HEIGHT 18 in (45 cm)
SPREAD 12 in (30 cm)
FLOWERING Summer
TEMPERATURE Above 52°F (11°C)

A hybrid of *M.* Lady Snow and *M.* Second Love, this orchid has flattened oval pseudobulbs and soft, pale green leaves that can reach 10 in (25 cm) in length. Fragrant flowers, 3 in (8 cm) across, are produced on upright spikes. They are bright pink with large, flaring, orange blotches, edged with white toward the base of the lips, which are centrally marked with yellow. This orchid is very free-flowering if given the right conditions. Grow in small pots filled with standard orchid potting mix.

Veining on the petals is more conspicuous than on other orchids of this type.

ONCIDIUM

Following a thorough overhaul, using **DNA** profiling techniques, of how orchids are named, *Oncidium* has become a huge genus (though not the largest among the orchids). It now encompasses plants previously known as *Odontoglossum, Cochlioda, Mexicoa,* and *Miltonioides,* as well as their hybrids.

At the same time, some oncidiums have been transferred to other genera. These are elegant plants, producing airy sprays of dainty flowers, and many are easy to grow as houseplants. There are also some valuable miniatures, ideal for displaying in a terrarium or growing where space is limited.

MINIATURE ORCHIDS

Diminutive oncidiums are becoming increasingly popular as starter houseplants, and for good reason. Hybrids such *Oncidium* Twinkle grow to no more than 12 in (30 cm) high but still flower generously in early winter. These miniature plants favor a small, tight pot (around 3 in or 8 cm in diameter) and consequently tend to dry out quickly if you don't water regularly.

Oncidium **Twinkle** is available in white, red, and yellow forms.

ABOUT THESE PLANTS

Oncidiums are highly variable plants. The genus comprises around 520 species of evergreen, epiphytic, sympodial orchids, some of which are also capable of growing on rocks. They are endemic to various regions of the Americas, as far north as southern Florida, and down to Mexico, Peru, and Bolivia, with one species native to Brazil. They are found in diverse habitats, growing anywhere from sea level to high in the Andes.

These orchids have roughly oval to conical pseudobulbs that each produce one to three somewhat leathery leaves, which emerge from the tips of the pseudobulb. The leaves differ in shape and size between species. Flowering spikes, which can be tall or short, upright or arching, appear from the bases of pseudobulbs. The flowers vary greatly in color and shape. Some hybrids can carry 12 or more flowers on each spike; many are available that are capable of flowering throughout the year.

HOW TO GROW

Oncidiums are cool growing, needing a winter minimum temperature of 50°F (10°C) with a summer maximum of 75°F (24°C). Owing to their diversity in the wild, it can be tricky to generalize about how to grow them. However, most of the commercially available plants will be happy in small pots filled with epiphytic orchid potting mix; those that have more delicate roots prefer a finer grade of potting mix.

Place plants in bright, filtered light in spring and summer, and move them into full light over winter. Water freely in spring and summer, when they should be growing strongly. They appreciate high humidity, so mist often. Apply fertilizer at every third watering; use a high-nitrogen type when in full growth, and high-potassium when pseudobulbs are maturing. Move them to a position in full light in winter and reduce the regularity of watering to keep the potting mix barely moist.

REPOTTING AND PROPAGATION

Plants can be repotted when they fill their container and the new pseudobulbs reach the pot edge—usually every two to three years. Repot after flowering, when the new leaf shoots emerge. They can be divided at the same time and dormant back bulbs separated for growing on individually. Hybrids are normally most impressive if allowed to develop without regular division but can be repotted to refresh the potting mix in spring or late summer.

***Oncidium* Goldiana** is commonly known as the dancing lady orchid for the shape of its flowers.

O. ALEXANDRAE

HEIGHT 20 in (50 cm)
SPREAD 10 in (25 cm)
FLOWERING Winter
TEMPERATURE Above 50°F (10°C)

Formerly known as *Odontoglossum crispum*, this is a Colombian native that grows in forests at altitudes of 6,000–10,000 ft (1,800–3,000 m). It has roughly oval pseudobulbs, each producing narrow leaves some 16 in (40 cm) long. Its white flowers, 3¼ in (8 cm) across, have ruffled edges and are produced on spikes to 20 in (50 cm) long. The lips are centrally marked with yellow and have irregular red spots. Grow in medium pots filled with standard orchid potting mix.

This well-known species has been widely used in breeding programs.

O. CHEIROPHORUM

HEIGHT 8 in (20 cm)
SPREAD 12 in (30 cm)
FLOWERING Fall–winter
TEMPERATURE Above 50°F (10°C)

This species is found in Mexico, Colombia, Panama, and Costa Rica, where it grows in forests at elevations of 3,250–8,000 ft (1,000–2,500 m), often in full sun. Its pseudobulbs are roughly pear-shaped, each producing a single narrow leaf. Lemon-scented, waxy, gleaming yellow flowers, ¾ in (1.5 cm) across, are carried densely on erect to arching flower spikes, up to 12 in (30 cm) long. Grow in small pots filled with standard orchid potting mix.

Flowers are generously produced in long, tapering clusters.

O. JUNGLE MONARCH

HEIGHT 12–16 in (30–40 cm)
SPREAD 8 in (20 cm)
FLOWERING Spring–summer and winter
TEMPERATURE Above 54°F (10°C)

This hybrid was bred from the species *O. maculatum* (originating in Mexico, Guatemala, and Honduras) and *O. Debutante*. It has ridged, narrowly pear-shaped pseudobulbs and strappy, bright green leaves that initially grow straight up but arch with maturity. Upright spikes carry up to 20 fragrant, pale greenish-yellow flowers that reach a diameter of 2 in (5 cm). The blooms are irregularly blotched with mahogany red, and have white lips marked with pinkish red. The plants can flower twice a year. Grow in medium pots filled with standard orchid potting mix.

The flowers open virtually flat to reveal their complex markings.

O. LANCEANUM

HEIGHT 16 in (40 cm)
SPREAD 10 in (25 cm)
FLOWERING Spring–fall
TEMPERATURE Above 55°F (13°C)

This species is native to parts of Central and South America, where it is found at altitudes of 980–1,640 ft (300–500 m). Plants either lack pseudobulbs or have tiny ones. The leaves are thick and leathery and speckled with red-brown, while flowers, which are 2½ in (6 cm) across, are yellow, and heavily spotted with chocolate or purple brown. Lips are violet-purple, the color fading toward the edges. Grow these plants in medium pots filled with standard orchid potting mix.

Long-lasting, spicily fragrant, wax-textured flowers give this orchid great appeal.

O. MOUNT BINGHAM

HEIGHT 18 in (45 cm)
SPREAD 12 in (30 cm)
FLOWERING Any time
TEMPERATURE Above 50°F (10°C)

This hybrid of O. Marzorka and O. Ingera was formerly classified within the now defunct hybrid genus x *Odontioda*. Its red flowers, which measure 3½ in (9 cm) across, are edged with pink and marked centrally with yellow patches. The narrowly oval leaves reach lengths of around 4–6 in (10–15 cm). This orchid has itself been crossed with O. Cornelia to produce the hybrid O. Cornelius Bingham. Grow this plant in medium pots filled with standard orchid potting mix.

Frilled edges add to the appeal of the richly colored flowers.

O. SHARRY BABY

HEIGHT 32 in (80 cm)
SPREAD 20 in (50 cm)
FLOWERING Any time
TEMPERATURE Above 54°F (12°C)

This impressive hybrid of O. Jamie Sutton and O. Honolulu has endured in popularity since its introduction in the early 1980s. Large, roughly oval pseudobulbs produce pairs of broad, arching, dark green leaves. Branching, airy spikes carry an abundance of chocolate-scented, deep cherry red flowers, each tipped with white. This makes an excellent houseplant, given sufficient room to accommodate the flowering stems. Grow in medium to large pots filled with standard orchid potting mix.

Spectacular when in full flower, this is deservedly one of the most popular oncidiums.

O. SOTOANUM

HEIGHT 6 in (15 cm)
SPREAD 9 in (23 cm)
FLOWERING Fall
TEMPERATURE Above 55°F (13°C)

This species is native to southern Mexico, Guatemala, El Salvador, and Costa Rica, where it grows epiphytically in rainforests at altitudes up to 5,000 ft (1,500 m). It has roughly oval pseudobulbs with soft-textured, narrow leaves, 4–8 in (10–20 cm) long. Strongly arching stems, to 20 in (50 cm) long, produce numerous, fragrant, white or pink flowers, ¾ in (2 cm) across, with darker pink lips. Grow in a hanging basket filled with standard orchid potting mix or mounted on a piece of bark.

Sweetly-scented flowers hang down from the plant in generous clusters.

O. TIGRINUM

HEIGHT 18 in (45 cm)
SPREAD 12 in (30 cm)
FLOWERING Winter
TEMPERATURE Above 55°F (13°C)

This Mexican species is found on Pacific-facing slopes at elevations of 5,250–8,200 ft (1,600–2,500 m). It has spherical pseudobulbs, each with one or two strappy, leathery leaves, 12–20 in (30–50 cm) long. Stout, usually upright stems, some 3 ft (90 cm) tall or more, carry loose clusters of long-lasting, fragrant flowers around 2 in (5 cm) across. These are typically dark red-brown with large yellow lips. Grow in medium-size containers filled with standard orchid potting mix.

Strikingly marked flowers are freely produced, making an impressive display.

O. TWINKLE

HEIGHT 12 in (30 cm)
SPREAD 8 in (20 cm)
FLOWERING Fall (mainly)
TEMPERATURE Above 55°F (13°C)

This popular miniature orchid is a primary hybrid between *O. cheirophorum* and *O. sotoanum*, both species from Central and South America. It has small, roughly oval pseudobulbs, each with two or three upright, leathery leaves that may grow to 4 in (10 cm) long. It produces large quantities of fragrant, pink, yellow, or white, gleaming, wax-textured flowers, ½ in (1 cm) across, in clusters on upright to arching stems, 12 in (30 cm) long. Grow in small pots filled with standard orchid potting mix.

This diminutive orchid is easy to grow and produces abundant flowers.

ALICEARA 'TAHOMA GLACIER'

HEIGHT 12 in (30 cm)
SPREAD 10 in (25 cm)
FLOWERING Spring–summer
TEMPERATURE Above 12°C (54°F)

This plant has a complex heritage. Crossing *Brassia* and *Miltonia* produced *Bratonia*; a cross of *Bratonia* Cartagena and *Oncidium* Alaskan Sunset resulted in this hybrid, which thrives both in cool and intermediate conditions. It has oval pseudobulbs and lance-shaped leaves, 9 in (23 cm) long. Flowers are around 2 in (5 cm) across, colored ice-green blotched with dusky pink, and overlap in clusters on upright spikes. Grow in medium-size pots filled with standard orchid potting mix.

Pointed sepals and petals give the flowers a starlike appearance.

ONCIDOPSIS NELLY ISLER

HEIGHT 20 in (50 cm)
SPREAD 8 in (20 cm)
FLOWERING Fall
TEMPERATURE Above 55°F (13°C)

This vigorous orchid is an intergeneric hybrid between *Oncidopsis* Stefan Isler and *Miltoniopsis* Kensington; *Oncidopsis* itself is the product of crossing *Oncidium* and *Miltoniopsis*. The plant has roughly oval pseudobulbs, each producing two or three broad, strappy leaves, which are up to 8 in (20 cm) long. Its lemon-scented flowers are bright red, with yellow centers and spotted lips, and are produced in well-spaced clusters on upright stems, which reach 20 in (50 cm) in height. Grow in small pots filled with standard orchid potting mix.

This attractive plant makes an ideal subject for anyone new to orchid growing.

ONCOSTELE MIDNIGHT MIRACLES 'MASAI RED'

HEIGHT 12 in (30 cm)
SPREAD 10 in (25 cm)
FLOWERING Late fall–early summer
TEMPERATURE Above 55°F (13°C)

This orchid is an intergeneric hybrid between *Rhynchostele bictoniensis*, found in humid forests from Mexico to Central America, and *Oncidium cariniferum*, from mountain forests in Costa Rica, Panama, and Venezuela. It has broad, roughly oval pseudobulbs with sword-shaped leaves, 20 in (50 cm) long. Clusters of 11 to 15 dark red flowers appear over a long period. Grow in small containers filled with standard orchid potting mix.

A long flowering season makes this a very desirable orchid.

PAPHS AND PHRAGS

Often referred to as "slipper orchids," *Paphiopedilum* and *Phragmipedium* (the members of which are commonly called "paphs" and "phrags") are distinct genera but are usually lumped together because their flowers are so similar in form, **strikingly marked, and usually solitary. Paphs are suitable for growing in the average living room but phrags tend to be taller, so are usually better off in a greenhouse or conservatory that can comfortably accommodate them.**

ABOUT THESE PLANTS

Paphs and phrags are largely terrestrial evergreens that lack pseudobulbs. The genus *Paphiopedilum* comprises some 60 species, which grow from sea level up to more than 7,000 ft (2,000 m), ranging from India to China and southeast Asia. There are many hybrids. *Phragmipedium* is made up of 15–20 species, all found in Mexico and Central and South America, mainly at low altitudes. Some members of both genera can grow epiphytically or lithophytically. All have strappy, leathery leaves, but those of the paphs are more variable in color and are sometimes mottled with gray.

Flowers of plants in both genera are large and produced singly or sometimes in clusters, though never in great numbers. Despite the superficial similarity between the two genera, there are differences, and they will not hybridize. With paphs, the upper sepals can be dominant and showily marked, while with phrags, they are usually less conspicuous, but the petals are longer and narrower, sometimes twisting.

HOW TO GROW

Paphs with mottled leaves are largely intermediate growing, while plain-leaved types are more often adapted to lower temperatures. A winter minimum of around 50–59°F (10–15°C) and a summer maximum of 75°F (24°C) suits

COME INTO MY PARLOR ...

The characteristic "slippers" of paph and phrag flowers do not mark them as carnivorous plants, as many people think. Instead, markings on the sepals attract pollinators, which then fall into the slipper. They emerge from the pouch unscathed, but in the process pick up pollen grains on their backs. These are transferred to the next flower they enter. The upper sepal curves over the pouch, preventing rainwater from collecting within.

Form perfectly follows function in phragmipedium flowers.

most. Phrags are intermediate to warm growing, some needing a winter minimum of 59°F (15°C); they are tolerant of high summer temperatures.

Paphs and phrags can be grown in terrestrial orchid potting mix with added crushed bark, paphs doing best in pots that restrict their roots. Filter the light in summer and maintain humidity around the plants, but do not mist. Water freely, applying fertilizer at every third watering. Place in full light in winter. Water paphs more sparingly during that period, but don't let the potting mix dry out between waterings. Phrags should be kept moist throughout the year, and feeding can continue in fall–winter, at six- to eight-week intervals.

REPOTTING AND PROPAGATION

Paphs and phrags should be repotted only when absolutely necessary—when plants reach the edge of the pot and growth is constricted: once every two to three years is normal. Remove all the old potting mix from around the roots and replace with fresh; cut off any withered or damaged leaves. Neither paphs nor phrags can be propagated by division, but both will occasionally produce offshoots (keikis) that can be removed for growing on (see p.44). This is best done after flowering, when a new leaf shoot appears.

Paphiopedilum flowers are often beautifully mottled or striped.

PAPH. APPLETONIANUM

HEIGHT 12 in (30 cm)
SPREAD 6 in (15 cm)
FLOWERING Winter–spring
TEMPERATURE Above 55°F (13°C)

This species originates from Laos, Thailand, and Cambodia, where it grows in deep shade in lowland evergreen forests and highland cloud forests at elevations of 2,300–6,500 ft (700–2,000 m). It has strappy, mottled, mid-green and purple leaves, to 8 in (20 cm) long. Solitary flowers, 4¾ in (12 cm) across, have slender, green, and rose pink petals, pale green upper sepals with darker veins, and light brown pouches. Grow in small pots filled with terrestrial orchid potting mix.

This paphiopedilum is among the easiest to grow, but must be watered generously.

PAPH. ARMENIACUM

HEIGHT 12 in (30 cm)
SPREAD 8 in (20 cm)
FLOWERING Spring–summer
TEMPERATURE Above 55°F (13°C)

This species is native to southwest China, where it occasionally grows on rocks, spreading laterally by means of creeping horizontal stems. Leaves, to 4¾ in (12 cm) long, are a marbled blue-green above and spotted purple on their undersides. Borne singly on stems up to 10¼ in (26 cm) long, the flowers, which grow to 3½ in (9 cm) across, are bright golden yellow. The pouches are thin-textured and dotted with purple within. Grow in small to medium pots filled with terrestrial orchid potting mix.

The gleaming yellow flowers are exceptionally large in relation to the plant.

PAPH. BELLATULUM

HEIGHT 4¾ in (12 cm)
SPREAD 8 in (20 cm)
FLOWERING Spring
TEMPERATURE Above 55°F (13°C)

This species occurs naturally in Burma and Thailand, where it favors moist, shady spots at altitudes of 1,000–5,250 ft (300–1,600 m). It has rigid, leathery, strappy leaves, to 6 in (15 cm) long, which are mottled green and gray. Very short stems carry solitary, rounded, white or pale yellow flowers, up to 3½ in (9 cm) across, which are heavily spotted with dark red. Grow in small pots filled with terrestrial orchid potting mix. For the best results, feed and water throughout the year.

The form of the flowers has given this paph the common name "egg-in-a-nest."

PAPH. CALLOSUM

HEIGHT 12 in (30 cm)
SPREAD 6 in (15 cm)
FLOWERING Spring
TEMPERATURE Above 55°F (13°C)

Native to Thailand, Cambodia, and
southern Vietnam, this orchid grows in
evergreen forests and sheltered, mossy
spots among rocks at altitudes of
1,000–6,500 ft (300–2,000 m). It has
strappy, grayish-green leaves, to 10 in
(25 cm) long, mottled with dark green.
Solitary maroon and green flowers,
2¾–3½ in (7–9 cm) across, have white
sepals, strongly striped with maroon,
and maroon pouches. Grow these
orchids in small pots filled with
terrestrial orchid potting mix.

Easy to grow, this species has striking
flowers and attractive mottled leaves.

PAPH. CONCOLOR

HEIGHT 6 in (15 cm)
SPREAD 8 in (20 cm)
FLOWERING Spring and fall
TEMPERATURE Above 55°F (13°C)

This species is found in southern
China, Thailand, and southern and
central Vietnam, where it generally
grows in lowland areas below 1,000 ft
(300 m). Its dark green and gray-green
mottled leaves extend to 6 in (15 cm)
long. Flowers, 3 in (7 cm) across, are
carried singly or in pairs on stems that
may be up to 4 in (10 cm) long. The
blooms are creamy white to soft
peachy yellow, and are generously
speckled with dark red. Grow in
small pots filled with terrestrial
orchid potting mix.

The flowers are slow to open, but may
last eight weeks on the plant.

PAPH. DELENATII

HEIGHT 8 in (20 cm)
SPREAD 6 in (15 cm)
FLOWERING Spring
TEMPERATURE Above 55°F (13°C)

Discovered in 1913 by French soldiers in Vietnam, the species was thought to be extinct until its rediscovery in 1993. It grows at elevations of 2,600–4,265 ft (800–1,300 m) and has rigid, strappy leaves, 4–6 in (10–15 cm) long, that are mottled green and gray above and have purple undersides. Its fragrant, white flowers reach a diameter of around 3 in (8 cm): they have pink pouches and are produced singly or in pairs on upright stems. Grow in small pots filled with terrestrial orchid potting mix.

This compact orchid has flowers that give off an elusive honey-lemon scent.

PAPH. FAIRRIEANUM

HEIGHT 6 in (15 cm)
SPREAD 6 in (15 cm)
FLOWERING Fall
TEMPERATURE Above 50°F (10°C)

This orchid grows on high river banks and in forests (occasionally on rocks) in the Himalaya, northeast India, and Bhutan, and is found at elevations of 4,265–7,200 ft (1,300–2,200 m). It has strappy, dark green leaves that grow to lengths of 3½–6 in (9–15 cm). Flowers are solitary and 2½–3¼ in (6–8 cm) across. They are pale greenish-white, veined with purple, and have greenish yellow pouches suffused with purple-brown. Grow in small pots filled with terrestrial orchid potting mix.

Unusually for paphs, flowers of this species are longer than they are wide.

PAPH. GOULTENIANUM 'ALBUM'

HEIGHT 12 in (30 cm)
SPREAD 8 in (20 cm)
FLOWERING Spring (usually)
TEMPERATURE Above 55°F (13°C)

Goultenianum is a hybrid group made by crossing *P. callosum* with *P. curtisii*—a species found exclusively in the leaf litter of coniferous forests of northern and western Sumatra. 'Album' is a selected form that has broadly oval, gray-green and dark green leaves reaching lengths of 4 in (10 cm). Solitary flowers, 4 in (10 cm) across, are lime green and white, with striped upper sepals. Grow in medium containers filled with standard orchid potting mix.

The fresh-looking flowers of this paph are strikingly marked.

PAPH. GRATRIXIANUM

HEIGHT 12 in (30 cm)
SPREAD 12 in (30 cm)
FLOWERING Fall–early winter
TEMPERATURE Above 55°F (13°C)

This species is found from Laos to Vietnam. It has strappy, firm, green leaves, to 12 in (30 cm) long. Flowers, 3 in (8 cm) across, are solitary and carried on upright stems, to 10 in (25 cm) tall, which arise from the center of the leaf rosette. The petals and pouch are glossy green, heavily veined with brown. The white upper sepal is spotted with brown or dark pink. Grow in small to medium pots filled with terrestrial orchid potting mix. Overwinter in a cool, dry spot to boost spring flowering.

The gleaming flowers of this species look almost as though they have been varnished.

PAPH. HAYNALDIANUM

HEIGHT 18 in (45 cm)
SPREAD 12 in (30 cm)
FLOWERING Spring
TEMPERATURE Above 55°F (13°C)

This species is found in the Philippines from sea level to elevations of 5,000 ft (1,500 m). It is a lithophyte or occasionally an epiphyte and has strappy, light green leaves that reach a length of around 16 in (40 cm). Flowers, 5 in (13 cm) across, are produced in clusters of up to six. They have green petals, tipped and spotted with rose pink, spotted upper sepals, and greenish brown pouches. Grow in medium to large pots filled with terrestrial orchid potting mix.

The elegant flowers of this species are held in loose clusters.

PAPH. MALIPOENSE

HEIGHT 20 in (50 cm)
SPREAD 10 in (25 cm)
FLOWERING Winter–spring
TEMPERATURE Above 55°F (13°C)

Native to southern China and Vietnam, this orchid was described as recently as 1984. It grows in cloud forests at altitudes of 1,500–4,750 ft (450–1,450 m), occasionally on rocks. It has broadly oval, leathery, mottled light and dark green leaves, to 6 in (15 cm) long. Hairy, upright stems, 12–20 in (30–50 cm) tall, carry raspberry-scented, bright green flowers, 3–4 in (7.5–10 cm) across, singly or (occasionally) in pairs. Flowers are lined and spotted with dark brown. Grow in small to medium containers filled with terrestrial orchid potting mix.

Tall flower stems carry the striking blooms of this rare orchid.

PAPH. MAUDIAE 'COLORATUM'

HEIGHT 12 in (30 cm)
SPREAD 6 in (15 cm)
FLOWERING Spring or summer
TEMPERATURE Above 55°F (13°C)

This orchid is a selected form of a group bred from *Paphiopedilum callosum* and *P. lawrenceanum*, which is found among limestone rocks and leaf litter in Borneo. It has roughly oval leaves that are mottled with light and dark green and reach lengths of around 4¾ in (12 cm). Its flowers are solitary and some 4 in (10 cm) across; they are a rich wine red, with strongly veined upper sepals and greenish white centers. Grow these plant in small pots filled with terrestrial orchid potting mix.

Individual orchids sold under this name may vary in their markings.

PAPH. MILLER'S DAUGHTER

HEIGHT 9 in (23 cm)
SPREAD 8 in (20 cm)
FLOWERING Spring (usually)
TEMPERATURE Above 55°F (13°C)

Miller's Daughter is a hybrid plant, bred from *Paphiopedilum* Chantal and *P.* Dusty Miller. It has strap-like, roughly oval, mid-green leaves, 6 in (15 cm) long. Its solitary flowers can grow to 4 in (10 cm) across; they have white petals and sepals that are sometimes flushed with creamy yellow. The blooms have pink veins and spots that merge into lines toward the middle. Pouches are white and pink, marked with yellow toward the center. Grow in small to medium pots filled with terrestrial orchid potting mix.

Flowers are carried well above the leaves on robust, upright stems.

PAPH. NIVEUM

HEIGHT 6 in (15 cm)
SPREAD 6 in (15 cm)
FLOWERING Summer
TEMPERATURE Above 55°F (13°C)

This diminutive species occurs in a range from southern Thailand to northern Malaysia. It has a very specific habitat, growing at low levels within humus-filled cracks in limestone cliffs. Over-collecting has made it rare in its natural habitat. It has very compact foliage; the rigid, leathery, strap-like leaves are just 4–6 in (10–15 cm) long and are mottled with green and gray. White flowers, 3 in (8 cm) across, have small red spots and are produced singly. Grow in small pots filled with terrestrial orchid potting mix.

While many paphs are somber-colored, *P. niveum* stands out for its gleaming white flowers.

PAPH. PINOCCHIO

HEIGHT 10–12 in (25–30 cm)
SPREAD 8 in (20 cm)
FLOWERING Any time
TEMPERATURE Above 55°F (13°C)

This paph is a primary hybrid of *P. glaucophyllum*, from southeast Asia, and *P. primulinum*, which occurs only in Sumatra. It has firm, strappy, rippled, bright green leaves. Flowers, to 4 in (10 cm) across, are solitary, and have bright green, heavily veined sepals and twisted, off-white petals that are bristly and spotted with burgundy. Pouches are pink, rimmed with yellow. Grow in small to medium pots filled with terrestrial orchid potting mix. Deadhead to encourage further flowering.

This hybrid paph is compact and easy to care for and can flower for several weeks.

PAPH. ROTHSCHILDIANUM

HEIGHT 24 in (60 cm)
SPREAD 18 in (45 cm)
FLOWERING Spring–summer
TEMPERATURE Above 55°F (13°C)

This species, found in the rainforests of northern Borneo at altitudes of 1,650–4,000 ft (500–1,200 m), has semirigid, strappy, glossy, mid-green leaves, to 20 in (50 cm) long. Flowers, to 8 in (20 cm) across, are produced in small clusters of two to six that are held above the leaves. The blooms have thin, purple-spotted, cream petals, white sepals that are spotted and striped dark purple, and purplish brown, yellow-rimmed pouches. Grow in large pots filled with terrestrial orchid potting mix.

With its boldly marked flowers, this is one of the most dramatic of all the paphs.

PAPH. SUKHAKULII

HEIGHT 6 in (15 cm)
SPREAD 6 in (15 cm)
FLOWERING Fall
TEMPERATURE Above 55°F (13°C)

This is a rare species, confined to small areas of Thailand at altitudes of 900–3,300 ft (240–1,000 m). It has narrow, mottled, dark gray and green leaves that reach lengths of 6 in (15 cm). Flowers, 4–4¾ in (10–12 cm) across, are produced singly. They have green petals that are heavily spotted with purplish black, white upper sepals striped with green, and reddish brown pouches. Grow in small pots filled with terrestrial orchid potting mix.

An endangered species, this plant is much sought after by collectors.

PAPH. THE EARL

HEIGHT 8 in (20 cm)
SPREAD 8 in (20 cm)
FLOWERING Winter
TEMPERATURE Above 55°F (13°C)

This clump-forming, hybrid paph was produced by crossing *P. oenanthum* with *P. petersianum*. It has strappy to narrowly oval, glossy, mid-green leaves, 8–12 in (20–30 cm) long. The flowers are produced singly, on upright, hairy, dark brown stems that emerge from the centers of the leaf rosettes. The blooms range from pale pink to a darker maroon; they grow to 3–4 in (7–10 cm) across, and are veined with wine red. Grow in small pots filled with terrestrial orchid potting mix.

Winter-flowering makes this plant very desirable to home growers.

PAPH. VANDA M. PEARMAN

HEIGHT 8 in (20 cm)
SPREAD 7 in (18 cm)
FLOWERING Spring–summer
TEMPERATURE Above 55°F (13°C)

This paph is a primary hybrid (a cross between two species) of *P. bellatulum* and *P. delenatii*, and was introduced in 1939. It has narrow, strappy leaves that grow to a length of 10 in (25 cm); these are mottled with gray and dark green above, and with purple on their undersides. The flowers are produced singly or in pairs and are 3½ in (9 cm) across; they are white with numerous burgundy spots and pink-flushed pouches. Grow in small pots filled with terrestrial orchid potting mix.

Often seen in collections, this paph has been the winner of several awards.

PAPH. VENUSTUM

HEIGHT 6 in (15 cm)
SPREAD 6 in (15 cm)
FLOWERING Winter–spring
TEMPERATURE Above 50°F (10°C)

These orchids are native to the Himalaya, where they grow at 3,300–5,000 ft (1,000–1,500 m), often within bamboo thickets near streams. Plants have broadly bladelike leaves, up to 10 in (25 cm) long; these are mottled gray-green and purple. The flowers, 3¼ in (8 cm) across, are produced singly. They have green and rose red, maroon-spotted petals, green-striped, white upper sepals, and yellowish-green to reddish-brown, prominently veined pouches. Grow in small pots filled with terrestrial orchid potting mix.

Bold markings on both the flowers and leaves give these paphs unique appeal.

PAPH. VILLOSUM

HEIGHT 6 in (15 cm)
SPREAD 6 in (15 cm)
FLOWERING Winter–spring
TEMPERATURE Above 55°F (13°C)

This species hails from northeast India, Burma, Thailand, and Laos. It has strappy mid-green leaves, 10–16 in (25–40 cm) long. Its flowers, some 3 in (8 cm) across, are produced singly. Held just above the foliage, they are glossy red-brown, with green and brown upper sepals and light yellow-bronze to green pouches. Grow in small pots filled with terrestrial orchid potting mix. This species is listed as vulnerable due to habitat degradation and over-collection.

Flowers of this species seem to gleam, resembling polished mahogany.

PHRAG. BESSEAE

HEIGHT 6 in (15 cm)
SPREAD 6 in (15 cm)
FLOWERING Spring
TEMPERATURE Above 57°F (14°C)

Discovered as recently as 1981, this species is native to the wet mountainous forests on the eastern slope of the Andes in Ecuador and Peru. It is also found growing on rocks. It produces rosettes of 6 to 10 strappy, leathery leaves, to 8 in (20 cm) in length, from a long rhizome. The bright scarlet flowers, 2½ in (6 cm) across, are produced singly or in small clusters. Grow in small pots filled with terrestrial orchid potting mix; water plants well—daily if possible—and support flower stems with stakes.

Bright, wet conditions favor this vividly colored orchid.

PHRAG. SEDENII

HEIGHT 24 in (60 cm)
SPREAD 24 in (60 cm)
FLOWERING Any time
TEMPERATURE Above 57°F (14°C)

This strong-growing phrag is a primary hybrid (a hybrid between two species) of *P. longifolium* from Costa Rica, Panama, Colombia, and Ecuador, and *P. schlimii*, which is found only in Colombia. It has strappy leaves that may be 12 in (30 cm) long. Upright spikes carry rounded, ivory white flowers, 2½ in (6 cm) across; these are delicately veined with pink. Petals are gently twisted and the rose-pink pouches are spotted on the inside. Grow in medium pots filled with terrestrial orchid potting mix.

A reliable grower, this hybrid phrag has long been popular with collectors.

PHALAENOPSIS

Members of this genus, often called "moth orchids," are the most common orchids in the plant trade. They are simple to grow and many a collection is based around these forgiving plants. No other orchids flower so freely and over such a long period, or are so tolerant of conditions in centrally heated homes. The plants are mostly compact and their huge color range means they can fit harmoniously into modern interiors. Some attractive miniatures can be grown even where space is at a premium.

ABOUT THESE PLANTS

More than 3,000 hybrids have been produced from the 63 species of *Phalaenopsis*—a testament to the popularity of the genus. These epiphytic, monopodial orchids are found in lowlands up to mountain forests in Africa, Madagascar, Asia, Indonesia, northern Australia, and the Pacific Islands.

Blooming at any time of year, they are elegant plants, with clusters of firm, dark green leaves, from the middle of which emerge tall, arching, sometimes branching flower stems. These carry clusters of rounded flowers that may overlap; their lips are often strongly contrasting and exquisitely marked. Plants tend to stay at a manageable size because old leaves at the base of the plant are shed when new leaves are produced. Roots often appear above the surface, and should be allowed to do so; they adhere to any surface they come into contact with.

HOW TO GROW

Phalaenopsis are mainly warm growing, needing a winter minimum temperature of around 59°F (15°C) and a summer maximum of 77°F (25°C). Plants will shed all their leaves if the winter temperatures fall too low.

Grow them in small pots filled with epiphytic orchid potting mix, though plants can also do well in rockwool. Surface roots can be exposed to the air. Some can be grown in hanging baskets or attached to bark rafts. Provide bright filtered light throughout the year, particularly when plants are in flower. From spring to fall, water freely and mist daily, applying fertilizer every four weeks. Water more sparingly in winter, avoiding wetting the leaves. Plants in bud should not be allowed to dry out but excessive watering during this period can lead to root rots. Stake flowering stems, which may break without support.

REPOTTING AND PROPAGATION

Repot when a plant's roots fill its pot. Do this when the plant is resting between flowerings (note that the presence of aerial roots does not necessarily indicate that the plant needs repotting). Cut off any dead aerial roots and remove withering leaves. Phalaenopsis are not suitable for division, but offsets can occasionally be removed from the base of the plant. Keikis that appear on the stems can be carefully removed and potted up separately in small pots once their root systems are well developed.

AN ORCHID FOR EVERYBODY

Phalaenopsis first became popular in orchid collections during the 19th century. Extensive hybridization and advances in propagation techniques in the latter part of the 20th century have resulted in a race of robust, reliable plants that now hold the largest market share of any commercially produced orchid. Globally, they are the second most popular flowering potted plant and, when sold as cut flowers, rival roses for their year-round availability, long vase life, and diversity of color.

A 19th-century lithograph of *Phalaenopsis schilleriana.*

Though very common in the plant trade, some phalaenopsis species are increasingly threatened in the wild.

P. ALLEGRIA

HEIGHT 3 ft (1 m)
SPREAD 18 in (45 cm)
FLOWERING Any time
TEMPERATURE Above 64°F (18°C)

A good choice for a bridal bouquet or corsage and one of the larger of its type, this moth orchid is common in the trade. It produces arching clusters of heavy, overlapping, pure white flowers with lips marked centrally with yellow. The bright green, leathery leaves can be up to 12 in (30 cm) long or more. It is a complex hybrid, its parents being P. Wilma Hughes and P. Alice Gloria. Grow in small pots filled with standard orchid potting mix; take care when watering to avoid splashing the open flowers.

Flowers are long-lasting and densely clustered on the stems.

P. CORNU-CERVI

HEIGHT 6 in (15 cm)
SPREAD 8 in (20 cm)
FLOWERING Any time
TEMPERATURE Above 64°F (18°C)

This diminutive species is found growing wild in a range that extends from Indochina to the Philippines. Its habitat is principally forests up to elevations of 2,460 ft (750 m). The fleshy, fragrant flowers, 2 in (5 cm) across, appear in clusters of three to five. They are yellow, blotched and barred with cinnamon red. The leathery leaves, 6–10 in (15–25 cm) long, are narrow and bright glossy green. Individual flowers remain open for up to four weeks. Grow in small pots filled with standard orchid potting mix.

The long-lasting flowers of this orchid are large relative to the size of the plant.

P. DORIS

HEIGHT 12 in (30 cm)
SPREAD 12 in (30 cm)
FLOWERING Any time
TEMPERATURE Above 64°F (18°C)

Produced by crossing *P.* Elisabethae with *P.* Katherine Siegwart, this compact orchid produces pink flowers, 3 in (8 cm) across, that have purple-red lips. They are held on arching stems that can be up to 3 ft (1 m) long. The broadly oval leaves are gray-green and up to 12 in (30 cm) in length. This free-flowering plant was bred in 1940 and continues to be popular thanks to its forgiving nature. It has been used as a parent of several newer hybrids. Grow in small pots filled with standard orchid potting mix.

Darker lips contrast well with the delicately shaded and veined petals.

P. GOLDEN HORIZON 'SUNRISE'

HEIGHT 6 in (15 cm)
SPREAD 12 in (30 cm)
FLOWERING Any time
TEMPERATURE Above 64°F (18°C)

This dainty hybrid is the product of a cross between *P.* Golden Buddha and *P.* Barbara Freed Saltzman. It has a spreading rather than upright habit. Its fleshy, creamy yellow flowers, 2½ in (6 cm) across, striped with red-brown and with orange-red lips, are carried on short stems to 6 in (15 cm) in length. The broadly oval, bright green leaves can be up to 10 in (25 cm) long. Needing more stable conditions than many other moth orchids, this plant is best suited to growers with some experience.

In good conditions, this orchid will flower up to three times a year.

P. LIPPEROSE

HEIGHT 3 ft (1 m)
SPREAD 12 in (30 cm)
FLOWERING All year
TEMPERATURE Above 64°F (18°C)

Created from a cross
between P. Ruby Wells and
P. Zada, this impressive hybrid
has warm pink flowers veined
with darker pink. Some 4 in
(10 cm) across, they are
carried on stems up to 3 ft
(1 m) long. The lips are white,
pink, and gold, with red
spotting and barring. The
bright green leaves are
broadly oval. This plant has
been widely used to produce
further pink-flowered hybrids
and is ideal for cutting for use
in floral design. Grow in small
pots filled with standard
orchid potting mix.

The exquisitely marked
flowers are produced in
generous quantities.

P. LUNDY

HEIGHT 6 in (15 cm)
SPREAD 3¼ in (8 cm)
FLOWERING Any time of year
TEMPERATURE Above 64°F (18°C)

Crossing P. Ella Fried with
P. Golden Amboin produced
this diminutive but striking
plant. The leaves are broad
and up to 9 in (23 cm) long.
Soft yellow flowers, large in
relation to the plant's size,
are 3¼ in (8 cm) across and
narrowly striped with red;
the stripes fork toward the
petal edges, creating a delta
effect. The plant should be
placed where the flowers
are backlit, so the delicate
petal markings can be
appreciated to the fullest.
Grow in small pots filled with
standard orchid potting mix.

Bold veining on the flowers
makes this one of the most
charming of the moth orchids.

P. SCHILLERIANA

HEIGHT 24 in (60 cm)
SPREAD 12 in (30 cm)
FLOWERING Winter and spring
TEMPERATURE Above 64°F (18°C)

Found in rainforests in the
Philippines at elevations to
1,475 ft (450 m), this species
produces an impressive
display of numerous showy,
faintly scented, rose pink
flowers. Some 2 in (5 cm)
across, they are held on
arching, branching stems up
to 3 ft (1 m) long. The broad,
fleshy leaves, to 18 in (45 cm)
long, are dark green, spotted,
and barred with silver-gray
on the upper surface. This
orchid is best grown in a
basket from which the
flowering stems can cascade
down to eye level.

With stems carrying up to
250 individual flowers, this plant
needs plenty of growing space.

P. STUARTIANA

HEIGHT 24 in (60 cm)
SPREAD 12 in (30 cm)
FLOWERING Winter
TEMPERATURE Above 64°F (18°C)

Native to the Philippines,
where it grows clinging to
trees in humid forests, this
intriguing orchid is notable for
its long leaves, to 14 in (35 cm),
that are mottled gray-green
on the upper surface and
have purple undersides.
The flowers, produced on a
branching stem up to 3 ft
(1 m) long, are white, the
lower sepals and lips marked
with yellow and dark maroon
spots. Out of flower, it is
similar in appearance to P.
schilleriana. Grow in small to
medium pots filled with
standard orchid potting mix.

The lower lip of each lightly
fragrant flower is curved like
a mustache.

'Alain Brochart' is a selected form of *P. schilleriana* with soft violet-pink flowers.

PLEIONE

These plants are a good choice for beginners because they are relatively simple to care for and tolerate cold better than most orchids. Numerous hybrids have been produced from the 20 or so *Pleione* species but they are quite similar, with elegant flowers mainly in the white–pink–lilac range. While a few can be grown outdoors in sheltered areas, they work best in an unheated greenhouse or conservatory, where they can take their place alongside rare bulbs and alpines to make an impressive display. They can be grown as houseplants, provided the summer temperatures do not rise too high.

ABOUT THESE PLANTS

Pleiones are deciduous orchids that, depending on species, may be terrestrial, epiphytic, or even grow on rocks. They are found mainly in wet forests at 3,250–13,000 ft (1,000–4,000 m), from northern India to southern China. Their pseudobulbs are short lived, and vary in shape; each produces one or two mid-green leaves, 6 in (15 cm) long, that are often shed before flowering. The flowers form on short stems at varying times of the year; they often have tubular lips with frilly margins.

HOW TO GROW

Pleiones are cool-growing, tolerating winter lows of just above freezing; a few can even withstand an occasional frost. Shallow-rooting, they are best grown in small, shallow pots filled with the appropriate potting mix.

In spring and summer, give them plenty of bright but indirect sun. Water freely, mist twice daily to raise the humidity, and feed at every third watering. When the leaves begin to die, reduce watering to keep the potting mix just moist and admit full light. If the temperature drops to freezing, stop watering and allow the plants to rest. Frost-tolerant species can be grown outdoors in mild areas but good drainage is essential.

Outdoor-grown plants make spectacular displays but may need protection from slugs.

REPOTTING AND PROPAGATION

Repotting is best done every year, in early spring before flowering, just as new shoots emerge. Remove and discard all the old potting mix and replace with fresh. For terrestrials, which need a growing medium that keeps roots moist in summer, houseplant potting mix mixed with perlite and fine bark can be used as an alternative to terrestrial orchid mix. Plants can be divided at the same time, if necessary, and old pseudobulbs can be discarded.

P. ALISHAN 'MERLIN'

HEIGHT 6 in (15 cm)
SPREAD 12 in (30 cm)
FLOWERING Spring
TEMPERATURE Above 34°F (1°C)

Alishan is a hybrid group produced by crossing *Pleione formosana* with *P. Versailles*. 'Merlin' is a selected form that has spherical to roughly oval pseudobulbs, each with a single leaf that grows to a length of around 6 in (15 cm). The flowers are borne singly; they are 3¼ in (8 cm) across and have mauve-pink sepals and petals with distinctive white tips. The white lips are frilled at the edges; the ridged interiors are yellow, marked with red-brown. Grow in shallow pots filled with standard orchid potting mix.

The bi-colored flowers of this hybrid distinguish it from other members of the genus.

P. BULBOCODIODES

HEIGHT 6 in (15 cm)
SPREAD 12 in (30 cm)
FLOWERING Spring
TEMPERATURE Above 34°F (1°C)

This terrestrial (sometimes lithophytic) plant is found in Burma and China, where it favors shrubby to thinly wooded slopes or damp cliffs at elevations of 3,000–12,000 ft (900–3,600 m). It has near-spherical pseudobulbs, each of which carries a single folded leaf that can reach 5½ in (14 cm) in length. Solitary flowers, 3 in (8 cm) across, are rose-lilac with white to pink lips that are spotted with pale brown or purplish pink. Grow in shallow pans of terrestrial orchid potting mix.

This orchid is known as the "Himalayan crocus" because of crocus-like appearance.

P. FORMOSANA

HEIGHT 6 in (15 cm)
SPREAD 12 in (30 cm)
FLOWERING Spring
TEMPERATURE Above 23°F (−5°C)

This terrestrial (sometimes lithophytic) species is found in eastern China. It grows in moist foggy areas near the tree line at altitudes of 5,000–8,000 ft (1,500–2,500 m). Each of its roughly spherical pseudobulbs produces a single leaf, up to 5½ in (14 cm) long. Flowers, 3¼ in (8 cm) across, are solitary. Pale rose-lilac, they have frilly-edged white lips that are margined with pink and blotched with brown or purplish pink inside. Grow in shallow pans filled with terrestrial orchid potting mix.

This delightful species is known as being one of the easiest orchids to grow.

P. SHANTUNG 'SILVER ANNIVERSARY'

HEIGHT 6 in (15 cm)
SPREAD 12 in (30 cm)
FLOWERING Spring
TEMPERATURE Above 34°F (1°C)

Shantung is a hybrid group produced by crossing *P.* × *confusa* (a naturally occurring hybrid of *P. forrestii* and *P. albiflora*) and *P. formosana*. 'Silver Anniversary' has conical pseudobulbs, each producing a single leaf that measures up to 6 in (15 cm) long. Flowers, 3 in (8 cm) across, have silvery white sepals and pink petals. The trumpetlike lips are pink and white, with frilled margins. The ridged insides are yellow, blotched with orange. Grow in shallow pots filled with standard orchid potting mix.

Flowers of this selected form of Shantung have a silvery cast, as the name suggests

PROSTHECHEA

The flowers of prosthecheas are unique among orchids because they are held upside down, with the lips upright at the top of the flower resembling a scallop shell and the petals and sepals hanging downward. This habit is clearly seen in *P. cochleata*, the national flower of Belize, sometimes known as the "octopus orchid" because its lower parts trail like tentacles. The flowers are very resistant to pests, particularly slugs, and last a long time on the plant. Largely undemanding, prosthecheas make excellent beginner or chids and are compact enough to grow almost anywhere.

ABOUT THESE PLANTS

These epiphytic, evergreen, sympodial orchids are found in the American tropics in moist woodland to altitudes of 8,530 ft (2,600 m). Widespread, they extend as far north as Florida. The pseudobulbs are somewhat elongated and often flattened, and each produces one to five strappy, leathery leaves. The sometimes fragrant flowers appear in clusters from the tips of pseudobulbs. The plants are toxic and should never be ingested.

HOW TO GROW

Prosthecheas are mainly intermediate growing, needing a winter minimum temperature of 52–54°F (11–12°C) and a summer maximum of 86°F (30°C). Place plants in a well-lit position, screened from direct light (especially important in summer). Water them sparingly but regularly from spring to fall, so the potting mix does not dry out. Regular misting can help keep the plants adequately moist and cool. Add a fertilizer at every third or fourth watering; use a high-nitrogen type while the new pseudobulbs are forming then a high-potassium feed to firm them up and encourage good flowering. Keep plants dry in winter (unless they are flowering, when the potting mix should be kept just moist).

Vespa **means** "wasp," and the flowers of *Prosthechea vespa* do indeed swarm on the plant like flighted insects.

REPOTTING AND PROPAGATION

Plants can be repotted when the roots fill the container and the pseudobulbs reach the edge of the pot. This is usually best carried out just after flowering (or in spring for *P. cochleata*), as new leaf shoots are starting to emerge. Repotting will probably be necessary every two to three years. Use standard coarse- or medium-grade orchid potting mix. Plants can also be divided at the same time. Dormant back bulbs can be separated from the plant for potting up and growing on separately.

P. COCHLEATA

HEIGHT 18 in (45 cm)
SPREAD 18 in (45 cm)
FLOWERING Any time
TEMPERATURE Above 52°F (11°C)

This species occurs from Florida to Mexico, Colombia, and Venezuela. It has flattened, roughly pear-shaped pseudobulbs and strappy leaves, around 8–14 in (20–35 cm) long. Ribbonlike flowers, 4 in (10 cm) long, are produced on spikes to 20 in (50 cm) in length. They have twisting, pale green petals and sepals and dark purple lips flushed with yellowish green. The white bases are veined deep purple. They are best grown in a slatted basket filled with standard orchid potting mix.

A well-grown P. cochleata plant will be almost constantly in bloom.

P. RADIATA

HEIGHT 8 in (20 cm)
SPREAD 12 in (30 cm)
FLOWERING Fall–winter
TEMPERATURE Above 52°F (11°C)

Native to central and southern Mexico, Guatemala, Honduras, and Costa Rica, this orchid grows in forests at altitudes of 500–6,500 ft (150–2,000 m). It has roughly oval pseudobulbs and strappy leaves that reach lengths of 14 in (35 cm). Spikes, up to 8 in (20 cm) long, carry fragrant, cream or greenish-white flowers that are typically 1⅜ in (3.5 cm) across. The lips, held uppermost, are striped with bright violet. They are best grown in a slatted basket filled with standard orchid potting mix.

P. radiata is a robust plant with beautifully formed, waxy flowers

PLEUROTHALLIS RESTREPIOIDES

HEIGHT 12 in (30 cm)
SPREAD 8 in (20 cm)
FLOWERING Winter
TEMPERATURE Above 50°F (10°C)

This epiphytic plant grows in cloud forests from Colombia to Peru. Lacking pseudobulbs, it forms clumps of upright, thick-textured leaves, each up to 10 in (25 cm) long. Arching flower spikes, to 12 in (30 cm) long, carry numerous purple-spotted flowers, to 1½ in (3.5 cm) long. Grow in medium pots filled with sphagnum moss (or an alternative) to retain moisture; place the pots in shade to avoid the heat in summer; water all year round.

The flowers are produced on one side of the spike, which stretches outward.

PSYCHOPSIS PAPILIO

HEIGHT 24 in (60 cm)
SPREAD 12 in (30 cm)
FLOWERING Any time
TEMPERATURE Above 50°F (10°C)

This cool growing, epiphytic species is from Trinidad, Venezuela, Colombia, Ecuador, and Peru. It has rounded pseudobulbs, each with a single leaf about 4¾–10 in (12–25 cm) long. Orange flowers, 6 in (15 cm) across, are carried on stems 4 ft (1.2 m) in length. The blooms are mottled with greenish-yellow and have yellow and brown mottled lips. Grow in standard orchid potting mix or on a bark slab. Place in full light and water sparingly; mist to maintain moisture in the summer.

Flowers that seem to hover have led to this being called the "butterfly orchid."

ROSSIOGLOSSUM

Formerly included within the now defunct genus *Odontoglossum*, rossioglossums now form a genus of their own, though it is small, numbering just six species. Vividly colored and often beautifully patterned, they are all highly desirable. Compact and easy to grow, they are excellent house plants, their winter flowering making them particularly valuable. They are reluctant to hybridize and cannot be crossed with any other genus. Possibly for that reason, rossioglossums are less widely seen in commerce than many other orchids.

Plants are best displayed so their brilliant flowers hang at eye level.

With their vividly colored flowers, rossioglossums deserve to be more widely grown.

ABOUT THESE PLANTS

Rossioglossums are sympodial, evergreen, epiphytic orchids found in the cloud forests of Central America, where they grow at altitudes of up to 9,000 ft (2,700 m). They have conical to roughly oval, compressed, dark gray-green pseudobulbs. From the tip of each appear one to three roughly oval leaves that are dark gray-green or bluish green. New leaves are peppered with brown. Eye-catching red and brown flowers are produced on upright to arching stems that grow from the bases of pseudobulbs.

HOW TO GROW

Rossioglossums are cool growing, needing a minimum winter temperature of 50°F (10°C) with a summer maximum of 86°F (30°C). They prefer a position in bright filtered light. Ventilate them well, and, in summer, water them freely, adding fertilizer at every third watering. Keep them dry in winter but watch the pseudobulbs; if they show signs of shriveling, apply enough water to plump them up again. Additions of sphagnum moss (or an alternative) or leaf mold to standard orchid potting mix can help keep roots moist, but take care not to over-wet the potting mix at any time. Best results may be achieved by growing the plants in hanging wooden baskets or rafts that allow for rapid drainage and maximum air movement around the plant.

REPOTTING AND PROPAGATION

Repot plants when the roots fill the pot. Do this every year or every other year to prevent the potting mix becoming stale. Plants can also be divided at the same time; firm, healthy back bulbs can be removed for growing on separately.

R. GRANDE

HEIGHT 14 in (35 cm)
SPREAD 12 in (30 cm)
FLOWERING Late fall–winter
TEMPERATURE Above 50°F (10°C)

Native to Guatemala, Belize, and Mexico, this species has clustered, oval to round pseudobulbs, each carrying one to three gray-green leaves. Spikes, to 12 in (30 cm) long, bear clusters of two to eight flowers, 6 in (15 cm) across. Sepals are yellow, marked with brown; wavy-edged petals are half yellow, half deep red-brown. Creamy white lips are marked with brown. Grow in medium-size pots or hanging baskets filled with standard orchid potting mix.

The waxy, long-lasting flowers are formed in late fall and winter.

R. RAWDON JESTER

HEIGHT 14 in (35 cm)
SPREAD 8 in (20 cm)
FLOWERING Fall–winter
TEMPERATURE Above 50°F (10°C)

This primary hybrid resulted from a cross between *R. grande* and *R. williamsianum* (an epiphyte from Mexico and Guatemala). It has bladelike, leathery, dark or bluish green leaves, 4–8 in (10–20 cm) long. Glossy, rich chestnut brown and yellow flowers, 4¾ in (12 cm) across, are spotted with red, brown, or yellow and have white lips. Grow in medium-size pots or hanging baskets filled with standard orchid potting mix.

A mature Rawdon Jester can flower twice a year if kept well.

STANHOPEA GRAVEOLENS

HEIGHT 24 in (60 cm)
SPREAD 12 in (30 cm)
FLOWERING Spring–summer
TEMPERATURE Above 59°F (15°C)

This is an intermediate growing, primarily epiphytic species sometimes seen on rocks. It is native to Mexico, Guatemala, Brazil, and Honduras where it is found in forests at elevations up to 8,850 ft (2,700 m). It has roughly oval pseudobulbs and upright, dark green, leathery leaves, to 20 in (50 cm) long. Trailing stems produce downward-facing, waxy blooms, to 5 in (12 cm) across, that are bright yellow with orange centers. Grow in a hanging basket filled with standard orchid potting mix.

The musky-scented flowers are individually short-lived but are often produced in succession.

THUNIA GATTONENSIS

HEIGHT 32 in (80 cm)
SPREAD 12 in (30 cm)
FLOWERING Summer
TEMPERATURE Above 50°F (10°C)

Thunia is a genus of deciduous, terrestrial orchids from the mountains of India, China, and southeast Asia. This hybrid is a cross of two species—*T. majoriana* and *T. winniana*. It has no pseudobulbs, producing clumps of upright to arching, bladelike leaves. Starlike flowers, 5½ in (14 cm) across, are white with flaring, pink, frilly lips stained yellow within and generously veined with red. Grow in terrestrial growing mix in medium-size pots.

Though breathtakingly beautiful and fragrant, *Thunia* flowers are not long lasting.

VANDA

With their vividly colored flowers, vandas are increasingly popular in floral design and have become the most widely grown of the monopodial orchids. There are now many hybrids, most produced by growers in the tropics. The flowers can make a dramatic contribution to a bridal bouquet.

The plants have prominent, stout, aerial roots and can be grown without any potting mix, either suspended in the air, or perhaps even more effectively, displayed in glass vases. They are equally at home in a well-lit living room or conservatory, provided they can be misted frequently.

ABOUT THESE PLANTS

Following DNA studies, botanists have expanded the genus *Vanda* to include around 80 species, some previously ascribed to other genera. These plants are found growing epiphytically in scrub forests at altitudes of 4,900 ft (1,500 m), from India to southeast Asia and Australia. They have thick, succulent, leathery leaves that fan out from a stout, upright stem. Thick, fleshy roots at the base of the plant are adapted to permanent exposure to the air.

HOW TO GROW

Vandas are intermediate to warm growing orchids, needing a winter minimum of 55°F (13°C) and a summer maximum of 86°F (30°C). They do best in hanging baskets filled with standard epiphytic orchid potting mix, or attached to pieces of bark. Alternatively, the whole plant can be suspended in the air using a length of fishing line. Water weekly in spring and summer, and every two to three weeks in fall–winter (immersing roots in water is the most efficient method). Mist aerial roots daily. For plants grown in glass vases, pour water over the roots once a week, then pour this out after 10 minutes. Add fertilizer at every second or third watering in spring and summer. These plants need good light year-round.

Producing an abundance of richly colored flowers, vandas are deservedly popular with florists and amateur growers.

REPOTTING AND PROPAGATION

Vandas can be repotted after flowering, if necessary, every two to three years, though this is more to renew the potting mix than to reduce congestion in the container. Plants are unsuitable for division, but offsets may sometimes appear at the base of the plant; these can be removed and potted up separately. Cuttings of stem sections can be rooted in spring. Keikis (see p.44) sometimes appear where the stems arise from the leaves. These can be removed once they have developed a good root system.

V. BLUE MAGIC

HEIGHT 24 in (60 cm)
SPREAD 16 in (40 cm)
FLOWERING Spring–summer but also at other times
TEMPERATURE Above 64°F (18°C)

Crossing V. Janet Hiddleston with V. Rothschildiana produced this popular, free-flowering hybrid. When well grown, flower stems can extend up to 40 in (100 cm) in length. They carry large numbers of rich violet-blue flowers, 4 in (10 cm) across or more, that are mottled with white. Plants grown commercially for floristry can flower at any time of year. Grow them in slatted baskets filled with standard orchid potting mix, attached to slabs of bark, or in a glass vase.

Blue Magic is a reliable orchid that can be in flower for up to three months at a time.

V. ROTHSCHILDIANA

HEIGHT 24 in (60 cm)
SPREAD 12 in (30 cm)
FLOWERING All year (intermittently)
TEMPERATURE Above 55°F (13°C)

This is a primary hybrid between V. sanderiana, from the Philippines, and V. caerulea, from India, Burma, Thailand, and China. Its thick-textured, curving leaves are 6 in (15 cm) long. Violet-blue flowers, 4 in (10 cm) across, are produced in long, drooping clusters; several of these clusters may develop and then flower simultaneously, sometimes twice or three times a year. Grow in slatted baskets filled with standard orchid potting mix or attached to slabs of bark.

Rothschildiana's plentiful violet-blue flowers are patterned with dark blue veins.

ZYGOPETALUM MACKAYI

HEIGHT 12 in (30 cm)
SPREAD 18 in (45 cm)

FLOWERING Fall–winter
TEMPERATURE Above 52°F (11°C)

Zygopetalum is a genus comprising some 20 evergreen species that grow epiphytically, in the ground, and occasionally on rocky outcrops in warm, moist rainforest regions of South America. There are several attractive hybrids, some with strong scents. All are easy to grow; some miniatures are suitable for windowsill culture, while larger types are better in a greenhouse or conservatory.

Z. mackayi is one of the most widely grown Zygopetalum species. It is a spectacular plant found in coastal regions of Brazil. It has fleshy, roughly oval pseudobulbs, each with two or three leathery, lance-shaped leaves, 12–20 in (30–50 cm) long. Upright stems carry clusters of five to seven sweetly scented, wax-textured, green flowers,

to 3 in (8 cm) across. They are strongly barred with brown, and have heavily veined, indigo-blue lips.

HOW TO GROW These are intermediate growing orchids. Grow them in medium-size, shallow pots (they do not like deep containers) filled with standard orchid potting mix. Place them in indirect light in spring and summer and move them into full light in winter.

Water and feed plants throughout the year, weekly in spring and summer, and every two or three weeks at other times. Make sure that pots are well drained as these orchids will not stand waterlogging. The plants are prone to leaf spotting, so water with care. Plants can flourish if crowded in their pots or can be divided immediately after flowering.

The decoratively patterned flowers are long-lived on the plant and are excellent for cutting.

INDEX

Author Andrew Mikolajski

AUTHOR ACKNOWLEDGMENTS

The author would like to thank Marek Walisiewicz who brought this project to fruition with unfailing patience and good sense.

PUBLISHER ACKNOWLEDGMENTS

DK would like to thank Mary-Clare Jerram for developing the original concept; Vanessa Bird for indexing; Diana Vowles for proofreading; Sara Rittershausen and all the staff at Burnham Nurseries, Newton Abbot, Devon (www.orchids.uk.com) for assistance with photography; and Paul Reid, Marek Walisiewicz, and the Cobalt team for their hard work in putting this book together.

PICTURE CREDITS

The publisher would like to thank the following for their kind permission to reproduce their photographs:

Alamy Stock Photo: Aaron Bastin 50bl; Adrian Sherratt 38tr; agefotostock 62cl, 78tl, 135tr; Alan Gregg 103tl, 135bl; Album 126bc; Alla Machutt 29tl; Allen Creative / Steve Allen 117c; Anant Kasetsinsombut 12br; Avalon.red 39tc, 95tr, 95bl, 96cr, 100cr, 103bl, 105tr, 105br, 119br, 122br, 134tr, 135tl; BIOSPHOTO 41tr, 52br, 58cr, 85c, 86tl, 94cl, 114br, 130bl, 131cl; blickwinkel 9c, 25cr, 70tl, 70br, 99tr, 104tr, 107tr, 125br, 135br; Botany vision 24bc; Budimir Jevtic 31bl; CaterinaTri 32c; Chirasak Tolertmongkol 14bc; CHRIS BOSWORTH 93cl; Chris Howes/Wild Places Photography 66bc; Chris Mattison 88br; Christian Musat 53br; Christopher Price 19tl; Chuck Place 98cl; Clare Gainey 82tr; CPA Media Pte Ltd 76bl; Crystite RF 11tr; Daniel Borzynski 118br; Danny Ye 59br; David Osborn 16br; Debbie Jolliff 15tl; Denis Crawford 53tr; Diego Grandi 13bl; Dorling Kindersley ltd 97tl; EDU Vision 65tl; Fcerez 51bl; Gekko Studios 29tr; Genevieve Vallee 81tr; Gerry Bishop 11bl; Gillian Pullinger 11tl; Gina Kelly 70tr; GreenSc 102tr; Gulsina Shaina 110bl; Hhelene 132cr; Image Professionals GmbH 57tl; imageBROKER 60tr; imageBROKER.com GmbH & Co. KG 116tr; Jacky Parker 2c; James Talalay 30bl; John Richmond 54c, 62tr, 135tr; John Swithinbank 49br; Jonathan Cohen 27cr, 27br; June green 119tl; Keith Larby 23tc; Kevin Schafer 139br; Khairil Azhar Junos 102cl; Kjell Sandved 13tl; Levente Bodo 35br; Lucy Griffiths 79tl; Maksim Kostenko 49bl; Mariia Boiko 4c; Marli Wakeling 98tr; Martin Fowler 75tr, 90bl, 103br, 112br; Martin Hughes-Jones 80bl; mauritius images GmbH 59bl; Michael Preston 84br; 91br; Mike Booth 18br; 61tr; 92bl; 97bl; 118tr; MikeCS images 69tr; Mim Friday 107bl, 123tl; Nadya So 35cl; Narinnate Mekkajorn 112tr; Natural Garden Images 128tr; Nature Picture Library 63bl; Nigel Cattlin 16cl, 49tr, 50tr, 51tl, 52tr, 53tl; Oleksii Shynkevych 53bl; Organica 57bl, 101tr; Panther Media GmbH 121tr; Peter Fields 123tr; Photo 12 130tr; Prakaymas vitchitchalao 138cr; Ray Wilson 135tl; REDA &CO srl 61bl, 63tl, 69bl, 75br, 105tl, 113tr, 121bl, 134cl; RM Floral 63tr, 106cr, 113br; Robert Kennett 88tr; Roberto Dziura Jr. 114bl; Ros Drinkwater 108tr; Ross Frid 56tr; Russotwins 50br; Sabena Jane Blackbird 90br; SFL Botanical 77c, 78tr; Steffen Hauser / botanikfoto 19tr, 75tl; Steve Tulley 12cl; Sue Bishop 17c; The Picture Art Collection 12bl; Tim Gainey 15br, 125tl; TommyK 118tl; Urs Hauenstein 60cl; WILDLIFE GmbH 95tl; Xinhua 8cl; Zena Elea 59tl, 61br, 120br; Zoonar GmbH 26c.

Bridgeman Images: Picture Alliance/DPA 29br.

Dorling Kindersley: 123RF.com: ariadna126 97br; Brian North / RHS Chelsea Flower Show 2009 61tl, 109bl, 139tl; Dreamstime.com: Whiskybottle 101tl; Mark Winwood / Alpine Garden Society 133bl; Mark Winwood / RHS Malvern Flower Show 2014 133tl, 133br; Mark Winwood / RHS Wisley 75bl, 124tl; Thomas Marent 63br, 89tr, 135br.

Dreamstime.com: Andrii Zorii 37tr; boonstocker 111c; Chirasak Tolertmongkol 124tr; Daniel Ripplinger 115br; Joloei 14br.

GAP Photos: Friedrich Strauss 71c; Howard Rice - St Barnabas Road, Cambridge 31tr; John Glover 87cl, 88bl, 115tr; John Swithinbank 52bl; Liz Every 86tr.

Garden World Images: Eric Crichton 79tr; Jenny Lilly 80tr; Sam Tran 135bl.

Getty Images: Barry Winiker 108bl; counterpoint / Imazins 64cl, 65tr; Fotografia de paisajes y naturaleza 6c; Jose A. Bernat Bacete 51br; Maria Mosolova 64tr; Pierre-Yves Babelon 56cl; The Asahi Shimbun 94tr; Vstock LLC 8br.

Getty Images / iStock: BakiBG 48bl; cyb3rking 67c; Farknot_Architect 104cl; gee1999 22bl; Hardt_E 90tr; joloei 20c; KseniaMay 27c; Mabelin Santos 51tr; NancyAyumi 74cl, 106tr, 114tl; Nilton Diaz 70bl; Photography By Tonelson 134cr; Probuxtor 28bl; RPFerreira 103tr; shihina 39br; Stanislav Sablin 25tr, 38cl, 46c; terra24 30cr; Volodymyr Kazhanov 34bl; Wachiraphorn 13cr, 42b; Zarina Lukash 49cl; Zingiber 120tl.

Naturepl.com: Juan Carlos Munoz 10br.

Science Photo Library: NEIL JOY 91tr.

Cover images: Front: GAP Photos: Visions Premium; **Back: Getty Images / iStock:** cyb3rking cl, joloei tr

Illustrations by Debbie Maizels

All other images © Dorling Kindersley

Produced for DK by
COBALT ID
www.cobaltid.co.uk

Editor Marek Walisiewicz
Senior US Editor Megan Douglass
US Consultant John Tullock
Managing Art Editor Paul Reid
Art Editor Darren Bland

DK LONDON

Project Editor Lucy Philpott
Assistant Editor Jasmin Lennie
Senior Designer Glenda Fisher
Editorial Manager Ruth O'Rourke
Senior Production Editor Tony Phipps
Production Controller Kariss Ainsworth
Jacket Designer Nicola Powling
Jacket Co-ordinator Abi Gain
Art Director Maxine Pedliham
Publishing Director Katie Cowan

Consultant Gardening Publisher Chris Young

First American Edition, 2024
Published in the United States by DK Publishing
1745 Broadway, 20th Floor, New York, NY 10019

A catalog record for this book
is available from the Library of Congress.
ISBN: 978-0-7440-9230-1

Printed and bound in China

www.dk.com